Advance

"As a highly va.......... ....*ured our quest to be a ...... of excellence in cultural competence. I highly recommend this book."*

—Elita Rosillo-Christiansen, Vice President
Cultural Competence/Diversity Officer
Inova Health System

"Every employee needs to know how to work and manage in a diverse environment. Tom's stories and examples translate diversity into action. A must-read for enhancing diversity skills and knowledge."

—Carolyn Jones, Senior Manager,
Corporate Diversity, Global Consulting Firm

"The 7 Clues for leaders in a multicultural world are wonderful 'common sense' guides for making better workplaces and for the joy of living. Are You Clueless? *is factual, informative, entertaining, and stimulating—a handbook to a better world for all who must find ways to work, play, and 'live together' or perish fragmented."*

"Reading Tom's book makes a better me, hopefully stimulating me to bring out the best in others."

—Edith Irby Jones, M.D., Past President,
National Medical Association

"Tom Finn's Clues help any woman or man to decode the gap between well-intended and culturally insensitive behavior and the often painful impact of that behavior. All of us who care about global peace can benefit from Tom's thoughtful and accessible work."

—Alexandra Merrill,
International women's leadership
development consultant

"Our communities and workplaces are becoming whole new worlds. Ah, but getting involvement, real motivation, and loyal, diverse customers? Here are some clues to make that happen, and some startling things we all may be missing."

—Catherine M. Hudgins,
Hunter Mill District Supervisor,
Fairfax County, Virginia

ARE YOU CLUELESS

7 CLUES
TO PROFIT, PRODUCTIVITY, & PARTNERSHIP FOR LEADERS IN A MULTICULTURAL WORLD

TOM FINN

KELLS
CASTLE
PRESS

ARE YOU CLUELESS?
7 Clues to Profit, Productivity, & Partnership
for Leaders in a Multicultural World

Copyright © 2007 by Tom Finn

Kells Castle Press
10866 Grovehampton Court
Reston, VA 20194-1432
info@areyouclueless.com

This book is sold with the understanding that the publisher and author are not engaged in rendering legal services. If legal or other expert assistance is required, the services of a competent professional should be sought. The author and Kells Castle Press specifically disclaim any liability that is incurred, or is alleged to have incurred, by the use of information contained in this book.

ISBN trade paperback 978-0-9797245-0-3
Library of Congress Control Number: 2007906789

Publisher's Cataloging-in-Publication Data

Finn, Tom, 1956-
    Are you clueless? : 7 clues to profit, productivity,
& partnership for leaders in a multicultural world / Tom Finn.
    p. cm.
    ISBN-13: 978-0-9797245-0-3
    ISBN-10: 0-9797245-0-3

    1. Diversity in the workplace. 2. Corporate culture.
3. Success in business.   I. Title.

    HF5549.5.M5F56 2007   658.3'008
                                     QBI07-600245

CREDITS
Copyediting: Ann Bruen   albruen@aol.com
                Deborah Costenbader   fdcostenbader@sbcglobal.net
Developmental Editing: Leslie Stephen   LeslieStephen@austin.rr.com
Cover and text design: Suzanne Pustejovsky Design   suzannep@austin.rr.com
Illustrations: Christopher Velez   demonfoxchris@yahoo.com
Logo Design: Michele Keen   mkeen@creativefreedom.com
Ninth Wave image: Lisa Laughy   llaughy@ninthwavedesigns.com
Author photo: Jim Kirby   www.jimkirbyphoto.com

First printing, October 2007

DEDICATION

To Dad, the one who would have
loved this the most.
And to the ones I love the most,
Kathleen and Mom.

The Ninth Wave

Lisa Laughy's image *The Ninth Wave* depicts the sea and its challenges using ancient Celtic symbolism, mermen, and serpents similar to those featured in the Book of Kells and Celtic mythology. To the ancient Celtic mind, the ninth wave out on the ocean was the symbolic boundary of the known world. To be forced to go beyond the ninth wave was to cross over to the unknown and to be exiled. Exile is a recurring theme throughout Irish history, and is well known to the multitude of Irish-Americans (and others) whose families have had to travel beyond the ninth wave.

Often, employees, customers, and community members know what it is like to "cross into the unknown" in our businesses, schools, agencies, and communities. The feeling and struggle associated with exile is similar to the stories diverse people tell in this book. "Exile" in organizations is familiar to the person whose idea has been rejected, the person with a foreign accent, the customer ignored because of her race, the person with a disability who sees no one like himself at the top, the woman executive who decides to leave a company because the environment stifles her progress.

The Ninth Wave symbolizes the struggle of exile. This book helps leaders ease all forms of exile, whether for customers or for employees in a company, agency, school, or community.

CONTENTS

Polish Your Points of Contact
Tip Sheet: Cross-Cultural Environment
   Building

Before You Start
Multiply Your Options
Check Your "Be" Before You Do

Ten Familiar Scenarios

PREFACE

THE ONLY THING I REMEMBER ABOUT the first dorm meeting of the first day of college was Lionel.

I was sitting across the room from a dark, unsmiling, big, black man. I came from an all-white, small town. I began to think I should meet Lionel—we were dorm mates, both freshmen, both new. Why not introduce myself?

But I was trembling. I was scared. With so little previous interaction with black people, all I had to go on were all the stereotypes and news reports. He was threatening to me, without doing or saying a thing.

Eventually I crossed the room. Eventually we were roommates and I the best man at his wedding. But that hesitation, and the internal energy I expended, is duplicated countless times every day across the United States and the world.

In over 20 years of consulting, I have seen that hesitation cost companies business, as culturally diverse customers decide not to approach. I have seen it bottle up employees who fear telling their bosses and organizations how their difference from the organization's majority groups influences their progress and productivity.

And this example is just about race. Consider all the different people you deal with in your business or agency, hospital or school—whatever your workplace. They may differ by age, language they speak, religion, sexual orientation, education, social class, nationality, and many other ways.

Do you honestly think you know what makes them all tick?

Do people representing all those differences knock on your door to buy your product, seek your mentoring, or help you accomplish your organization's goals?

Or are they waiting for you to "cross the room"?

The evidence in this book suggests that many leaders and organizations are clueless to culture's impact. That impact includes lost customers and profits, customers spreading bad news about your company, key talent going elsewhere, and employees having no clue how to handle multicultural situations. What don't we know—and how much can *knowing* pay off? See for yourself in the first part on "Faces of Cultural Cluelessness."

Are you clueless? The answer to that question, in a global world, could bring you new customers, solve your need for scarce talent, and resolve community and school conflicts. With a few Clues, that is.

INTRODUCTION

The Manager Is the Company

There are many books about making an *organization* culturally competent. This one targets a different level—the individual manager. *Are You Clueless?* addresses the leader who is in the middle of all the cultural shifts in today's workforce. It gives that leader ideas for things he or she can control every day.

My audience is the individual leader, but that target is just as influential as a company culture. I coach U.S. and overseas managers on how they can increase their capacity to influence. Time and again, when I ask, "What's it like to work here?" employees tell me, "It depends on your manager." Managers *are* the company or the agency, the school or the hospital. It's like in school, when a boring subject becomes exciting in the hands of a good teacher.

A woman I know works crazy hours. Initially, her job was uninspiring and a lot of work. Then she got a new boss who was innovative and wanted to use her skills and consult her. Voilà! Her "company" became a great place to work.

So, the question "Are you clueless?" contains some added punch when you consider our increasingly multicultural workplace. Would diverse employees say you lead "a great place to work"? Are you aware of how multicultural customers view your business or service?

The labor force and your customers or constituents include people with disabilities; gays, lesbians, bisexuals, and transsexuals; people from other countries; people of all religious faiths; people who speak another language; military and civilians; people with college degrees; and people from the school of hard knocks. Do you have the "cultural competence" to attract or inspire all these people? If the perception of the company depends on the manager, as employees tell me, then managers must create an organization that appeals to customers, employees, and constituents who differ widely.

Are You Clueless? reveals those customer and employee perspectives.

If I took you with me consulting, to hear customer and employee stories in Houma, Louisiana; Buenos Aires, Argentina; or Newark, New Jersey, you would see that there are patterns for managing across all the differences I have mentioned.

If I brought you with me to an oil company, an assisted-living center, a defense company, or a school, you would see the same behaviors at the top and the bottom, and you'd see cross-cultural strategies for bridging divides, whether they be class, race, gender, religion, or department to department.

I'll take you on those journeys and look at those strategies through the medium of this book.

Using This Book

The heart of *Are You Clueless?* is its 7 Clues, the essential skills needed by leaders who work with diverse workforces and customers. Those Clues are then applied to situations you may face as a leader every day.

Part One: Faces of Cultural Cluelessness sets the stage. It illustrates the astounding ways multicultural customers view, and are being treated by, our organizations. The need for the 7 Clues becomes clearer when our diverse customers tell their own stories.

Part Two: Clues for Cracking the Cultural Code introduces the 7 Clues for cracking the cultural codes in our workplaces. The first three Clues are foundational. Consider **Clue 1: Look to Your Organization's Cultural Guidelines** and **Clue 2: Turn to the Law** as backups for handling cross-cultural issues. They are official guideposts.

Clue 3: Clarify Your Cultural Lens demonstrates the value of knowing cultural influence on *self*. As Dr. Phil says, "Self Matters," but in ways related to cultural differences that many Americans and leaders around the world simply don't see. Unfortunately, many of your employees and customers *do* see the influence of your cultural background, so it behooves you to know the judgments they may be making.

Clue 4: Apply Cross-Cultural Patterns and **Clue 5: Use Group-Level Radar** zero in on the patterns that distinguish management of cultural differences from generic management. Knowing these patterns can help you shift situations that are stuck and give you a cultural lens that applies to the many differences that you likely manage.

The two remaining Clues combine those patterns and the three foundational Clues into two cultural competence strategies, one for individual performance improvement across differences, and the other for the organizational level.

Clue 6: Coach Performance Cross-Culturally takes the skill of coaching into a new dimension. This is coaching when you are dealing with people very different from you—a topic on which I have not seen a lot of coverage.

Clue 7: Build a Cross-Cultural Environment adds to the individual skills covered earlier in the book with suggestions for creating a workplace conducive to diversity. The idea here is that you not only pay heed to making a workplace attractive to a multicultural work-force, you also make your business attractive to in-creasingly diverse customers.

Part Three: Opportunities to Turn Clueless to Competent sets up some common cultural scenarios facing today's leaders and organizations. To give you guidelines for handling each situation, I suggest the Clues that best apply to each scenario. You may see some themes from earlier in the book repeated in the solutions to the situations. That's the idea: the funda-mental patterns and the 7 Clues apply, repeatedly, to varied scenarios. My hope is you find yourself saying, "Ah ha! The root of this problem is an Insider/Outsider dynamic. So here's what I do."

Part Four: Summing It All Up is a brief reminder of the ground we have covered and a call to action to start today to crack the cultural codes operating in your place of work.

Getting It . . . and Profiting

If you count all the different groups among your cus-tomers and employees, leaders in business, govern-ment, and communities have a major challenge. But

I contend that leaders can use knowledge about cultural patterns and apply those patterns to a host of differences, whether the situation involves a person from another country, a woman, a civilian, a person who speaks another language, someone from another part of the country, someone from another department, a gay man, or any other difference. You can be, to a great degree, culturally competent with many different "cultures" if you know your own cultural preferences and some universal patterns for managing differences.

I have written this book, however, because I see countless examples of what I would call "cultural cluelessness" on the news, in society, and in our organizations. We know, from Texaco, Denny's, Coca-Cola, and other high-profile cases, that it is easy for your customers and your employees to see you as culturally incompetent. Schools and communities, with multiple languages, nationalities, and religions, cry out for leaders who "get it."

Are You Clueless? gives you some guidelines and recommended practices for "getting it" culturally. In businesses and communities that are more multicultural every day, that understanding is a leader's route to profit, productivity, and partnership.

Reston, Virginia   *Tom Finn*
September 2007

PART ONE

Faces of Cultural Cluelessness

How Multicultural Customers See You

*In an effort to remain gender neutral, this book
alternates references to men and
women whenever possible.*

ARE YOU CLUELESS? Do you know how much you don't know . . . about what your customers want, what they aspire to, how they see you? Multiply whatever answer you came up with by plenty when you factor in your multicultural customers.

Brave New Managers

What's different about leading a multicultural workforce? What if you've heard it all about leadership, or read the leadership gurus: the Tom Peterses, the Rosabeth Moss Kanters, the Peter Druckers, the *Fast Company* magazines? Isn't leadership all the same, no matter what your workplace is like?

Maybe you should ask my customers:

1. A pharmacy department head who leads a department with

   - a female Iranian supervisor, who manages men who won't take direction from a woman

   - a virtual United Nations of a workforce (Africans, Middle Easterners, Latinos, blacks, rural and city-raised white Americans, 20-year-olds to 60-year-olds)

   - language cliques who spread gossip by speaking their own language, and co-workers who can't understand them feeling like they are deliberately excluded

2. A restaurant manager who cannot speak to a quarter of his workforce because he doesn't know their language.

3. A health care organization where fights occur among ethnic groups who have a history of conflict in their *native* country and have simply brought it into their workplace here in the United States.

4. The organizations that call me because "we're having race problems."

▶ *Brave new world? I'd say, brave new managers.*

Clueless to Profit and Productivity

Business leaders who lead businesses, changing communities, and government agencies can't use "one-size-fits-all" techniques and assumptions in the face of diversity. Yet the Druckers and the Peterses rarely talk about solving race problems or leading today's multicultural workforce and customer base.

Are You Clueless? gives managers some tools for responding to cultural variety in the workplace. But don't think you are off the cultural hook if you are managing in a virtually one-race or one-nationality organization, and you think you don't have "culture." Notice in the examples of language, race, gender, age, ethnicity, and regional differences above that I am using a broad definition of "culture" to describe the challenges today's leaders face.

Here is a working definition of culture:

"the behaviors, ideas, attitudes, values, beliefs, customs, language, and ceremonies of a people or group that are transferred, communicated, or passed along."

Take a good look at that definition. If groups have different behaviors "passed along," then men and women have different "cultures," if you will. Different behaviors, expectations, and attitudes get passed down to men and to women. What's more, different age groups, gays and heterosexuals, military and civilians—the list goes on—evolve their own sets of beliefs, values, and actions that pertain to their culture. As a leader, you are managing cultural differences even if your whole workforce is one race or nationality.

These subtler group differences—and the fact that leaders who are members of particular groups can't grow up knowing about all the others—make cultural competence harder. Yet many people think managing cultural differences is easy, saying, "I don't see the problem."

That's the issue: with culture, most often we don't know what we don't know. We don't see the problem.

So it's no surprise that women have called men "clueless" for years. Or that the T-shirt slogan, "It's a black thing, you wouldn't understand," makes perfect sense. I *wouldn't* understand—I'm not black.

So, when I ask, "Are you clueless?" part of that question is "What don't you know about your customer base—and potential profit—that is likely changing along with the demographic shifts in the country?"

Or, have you considered that employees may stay or leave, participate or remain silent and sullen, give their all or put in their time, because you either understand or are oblivious to their cultural motivators?

This book activates your cultural radar.

▶ **Get to know what you don't know . . . and profit.**

**God Knows How Many Diverse
Customers Stay Away**

*"By my calculations, 714 multicultural customers
avoided your business this year."*

A Bank for White People

A bank hired a female manager who spoke Spanish. As happens with so many businesses, she often became the resource to whom everyone would run when a Spanish speaker walked in, though that wasn't the position for which she was hired.

A Spanish-speaking couple came in. They didn't have an account. They were shopping for a bank.

Manager: *Have you been here before?*

Couple: *No.*

Manager: *And what brought you in today?*

Couple: *We heard you had someone who could speak Spanish. We never came in before because we thought you were a bank for white people.*

How many of the bank's employees do you think had been thinking, "Yup, we're a bank for white people?" I'm quite certain the bank didn't promote itself as "the number one bank for white people in our region!"

Looking in, though, from the customer's perspective, that is the image a Latino couple had. Consider who your customers are, by cultural group, and expand that definition of "culture" beyond ethnicity and national origin to people with disabilities, religious groups, gays and lesbians, military people, and foreign language speakers. Who is walking in your door . . . and who is not?

Then think about the simple step this bank took that brought in a new customer: Someone who spoke the customers' language became an employee.

▶ *See what diverse customers see.*

The Growth Story

NBA basketball great Magic Johnson, smiling all the way to the bank, continues to build theaters and shopping malls in African American communities where traditional retailers would not go. He is serving the underserved.

I'm not sure we're all getting the significance for business and government of the many cultural demographic shifts that are taking place. Consider, for example, national origin and languages spoken in the United States.

There are more than 28 million immigrants in the U.S.—a 43 percent increase since 1990.

Ten percent of the U.S. population is foreign-born. In my county, like a lot of other places, it's much more: 25 percent. One of every four people was born outside the United States!

If you want your business to grow, your school to excel, or your agency to succeed, identify the customer, student, and citizen segments that are growing. In one county outside Washington, D.C., the white population has declined by 22 percent since 1980. It's not that whites are fleeing—it's just that the growth of other racial and ethnic groups is so strong.

Consider just one implication: Many of the new immigrants have limited English proficiency. In the

Washington, D.C., region, more than 50 percent of Asians and Latinos report they speak English "less than very well."

Or reflect on the notion that some stereotypes about immigrants are just not true; in the D.C. area, for example, diversity there does not mean poverty. Many foreign-born residents have high incomes.

You say you live in Maine or North Dakota and you don't have these numbers? How about the co-workers you deal with from across the country who are different from you? What about the customers you have in other states or other countries? One manager in South Dakota leads a call center that works with na-tional and international clients. She notes that her work exposes her not only to different accents, regional cus-tomer styles, and demands, but also to lifestyles that people in her part of the country sometimes find objectionable.

What are you doing to track, appeal to, and serve these customers and citizens? What might you be doing that turns them off? What might your diverse employees know about these customers and citizens?

▶ *If you want your organization to grow, look at who's growing.*

"That's My Village!"

Some organizations *are* paying attention. Down to the smallest detail.

One health care system has become so aware of the importance of immigrant communities to its survival and mission that it tailors the artwork on its walls to its diverse customers. A Brazilian man stopped before one of the pictures and shouted, "That's my village!"

There is opposition at times to our increasing diversity; for example, some people object to signs in Spanish. Whatever your beliefs or fears personally, smart businesses are making money by making people like this Brazilian man feel more at home in his adopted home. Schools have no choice—the kids are diverse and the languages are diverse. On our street, Jack and Claire play with Ashkan, Sach, Abdullah, Sneha, and Sravya. They figure out how to communicate with Evie's grandparents, who can't speak English, but who have a fine time in the neighborhood because they can take walks with about five or six other sets of Chinese grandparents.

You may or may not like this picture. You may be in a position similar to the South Dakota call center manager, who comes from a community where many members object to different lifestyles or cultures, but who must lead a group that serves multiple cultures.

As a fact of life, your business, school, or agency is likely having to address its diverse customer or citizen base, and you as a leader may have to lead such efforts. What do you know about Indian parents' expectations for their child's education? Do you think women, a particular age group, gay and lesbian customers, might expand your sales if you addressed their needs? Do you think a potential customer will notice if an all-male team presents your jazzed-up presentation?

If you say no, how come a Brazilian man noticed a picture on a wall in a hospital in Massachusetts?

▶ *Are you sweating the cultural details?*
Read on.

Gaining 1,000 Customers

Here's an easy way to pick up 1,000 customers.

For one of my customers, let's call the company XYZ Health Care, I spoke with a group of 16 women who were members of a local Muslim foundation. They were asked to give their view of the health care system, which has several hospitals and other smaller clinics.

One of the women explained that her mother had a horrible experience at one of the system's hospitals.

> *Everyone in my family knows about that incident and they will never go to that hospital.*

On the other hand, she said, she had a wonderful experience at another of the system's hospitals, and she continually praised the good care and the people at that hospital.

> *Everyone in my family also knows about my good experience at that hospital.*

She made this statement, of course, in the company of the 15 other women, thus spreading the news again.

I was curious that she emphasized "everyone" in the family. I asked:

Q: *How many people are in your family?*

A: *Sixty-four that live around here.*

Q: *Sixty-four?*

A: *Well, yes, most of us have large families, and there are aunts and uncles and cousins . . .*

Q: *So you've talked to all 64 about your experiences with XYZ?*

A: *Oh, yes, they know about the bad one and the really good one.*

As she was saying this, all the 15 other nonrelated women nodded. I got more curious about the spread of information. Before I could ask, another woman piped up.

> *Yes, we tell each other everything—where to get a good haircut, where the sales are.*

I had already heard and seen, in touring the foundation, that this was not really a funding organization. There was a school and a large play area for kids.

> *We have gatherings most every week for families. Everybody comes.*

> Q: *About how many people come to the foundation for the gatherings?*

> A: *Oh . . . about 1,000.*

Just a little research and you will find that this kind of immediate, burgeoning networking is how it's done among culturally diverse ethnic, racial, religious, even gay and disability communities. Not everyone knows, for example, that there are gay yellow pages. The former head of U.S. Advertising for American Express and two marketing professors confirm that word-of-mouth is *the* method for reaching cultural groups.

A credit union manager in California says of the Latino community he serves: "This community is very word-of-mouth oriented. They trust only the people their family and friends trust."[1] In Boston, where one in four residents is an immigrant and where about 140 languages are spoken, word of mouth becomes the newcomer's "instant messaging."[2]

It makes sense. If you're different from the mainstream, there's something very comforting about gathering with those like you. There's also an easy leap to conversations about businesses that treat you well, and those that don't, because everyone understands what you go through everyday when you are different from the mainstream population.

▶ *Looking for customers who bring in customers? Impress a cultural network.*

Don't Talk to Security Guards

Like the Latino couple who avoided the Bank for White People, some people are not walking in your door. Many of the ones who do, however, are having experiences with your parking lot attendants, telephone operators, teachers, doctors, security personnel, and customer service employees that would baffle you or make you cringe.

Do you know the impact of what's going on outside your business's doors for diverse customers?

Two Cambodian women, one of them pregnant and a newcomer to the U.S., drove to a large hospital to inquire about obstetrical services. Driving in, they could not figure out from the signs where they could park.

They drove around for 20 minutes.

Finally, the woman who was driving said, "Why don't we ask a security guard?"

"No!" the pregnant woman insisted.

It seems the pregnant woman's experience with uniformed security people in her country was that they often killed people. She was not going to approach them.

This example is not really about security guards. The larger point is to understand that the pictures on your walls, the pace of conversation that you are used to, the forms you use, the signs you have, even your parking lot, may be a traumatic or stressful gauntlet to someone culturally different from you.

How do you deal with that?

It would be impossible to key all of your actions and procedures to the multiple cultures we now encounter in business. What is possible is simply to remember that diverse people often experience the same walls, forms, and environment differently than you do. In health care settings, my company has offered what we call "Mystery Patient" services, akin to retail's Mystery Shoppers, where we send diverse people to simply experience the hospital. The hospital then gets some inkling of how their parking lots and walls are having an impact on people who will increasingly become their bread and butter customers.

The other revolutionary thing you can do is ask.

▶ **Find out how diverse people experience the things you take for granted.**

The Danger of Head Nodding

We've all done it. You didn't quite hear someone and you act like you agree. You didn't get the joke and you laugh. You don't understand a word and you act like you do.

Harmless, interpersonally. Deadly to your business—potentially literally, in some cases.

Suppose you are living and working in another country, having to conduct your life in the home country's language. For most of us, the whole day would be a series of jokes missed, words we didn't understand, things we didn't quite hear.

Now think about your customers or potential customers whose first language is not English or who come from another country. Are all of them telling you what they would like? Are they questioning things they don't quite understand? Some may—and they can be loud and obnoxious just like any American retail customer.

Many others are like Spanish-speaking patients who are assisted by Spanish-speaking caseworkers in a large, diverse county. The caseworkers' primary role ends up being an "advocate." In other words, their role goes way beyond translating. They find that the major role they play is to get patients to assert themselves when meeting with a doctor or health care specialist.

It seems the cross-cultural interaction the patients have is blocked by far more than language, but the doctors and nurses are often totally oblivious to it. Many patients are intimidated by the professional level of the person treating them and simply go along, often not providing key information that would help the specialist treat their illness. Others don't understand the instructions to take medication at regular intervals—not from a language standpoint, but rather because they are not used to this. Others stop taking the medication because they feel better and don't want to spend the money. Still others feel they are treated poorly and dispassionately when they try to call or return for medications, so they stop calling rather than go through the experience.

Many of these—in some cases, life-threatening—situations happen because of head nods. The patients nod as though they understand and will follow up, and the specialists move on.

How many head nods are you getting? How many potential repeat customers are you losing because of experiences they are having further down the road with your business, brought on because your employees are not taking some small extra steps with diverse customers?

▶ **"Getting it," reversed. How do you know your diverse customers understand you?**

"Nice Doesn't Cut It" (Employee Cluelessness)

In one of our Mystery Patient assessments for a health care institution, we were treated with great courtesy at a few hospitals and in several departments. These employees had customer service excellence down.

Yet, many had no idea what to do with a "cultural challenge."

We posed this scenario:

My sister-in-law, who is from Gujarat, India, is pregnant, is Muslim, and speaks only Gujarati. We are looking at different hospitals to see who can best handle some of her needs related to religion, language, and culture. What do you do to deal with these needs?

In the lobby, they send me to their Ob-Gyn clinic.

Ask there, the receptionist says.

At the Ob-Gyn clinic, when I say my sister-in-law has insurance, they reply:

I don't know what to tell you. Go to Social Services.

At the Social Services Department, the receptionist is stumped.

The social workers are busy, she says.

After an awkward back and forth with her repeating, *I have no idea,* I volunteer:

Is there a Patient Relations Department?

Relieved, the receptionist says,

Yes! Go there.

In Patient Relations, I am treated warmly. I get some accurate information, but I also am told some things that may violate Federal guidelines regarding use of family members in medical translation.

Later I presented these and other findings to the hospital system's top administrators. They were aghast at the cultural cluelessness I encountered, starting with the first hospital employee I spoke to who referred me to the Ob-Gyn clinic on the assumption that a foreigner couldn't pay.

I repeated to one of them on a break that I would admit that I was treated very nicely. *"Nice doesn't cut it,"* she replied.

So true. In these and other examples, lack of employee knowledge risked making the customer's experience onerous, losing the customer, and even creating legal liability.

There is another hidden concern for leaders with multicultural customers: note in this example that receptionists are a primary contact for the customer. So are security guards and volunteers from the Ladies Auxiliary. Scandinavian Airlines saw a parallel to this years ago when its studies of customer contact showed that customers had an average of 15 seconds' contact with SAS people. Who was the only face of SAS for those 15 seconds? Ticket agents, baggage handlers, and receptionists.

So employees need to know how to handle cultural challenges . . . and the *right* employees need to know how to handle cultural challenges. Many of your customers judge your business through interaction with your lowest-paid or lowest-on-the-organizational-chart employees. Who is the face of your business, and what 15-second impression are those employees making on culturally diverse people?

Don't assume, again, that cultural encounters are limited to people from foreign countries. Employees need your support to properly handle cross-racial cultural encounters. Several residents in a nursing home facility refused to let a black employee touch them, though they needed help moving. A small diaper service found that a customer suddenly began objecting to the driver coming to pick up her delivery. She had never complained before, but the company had just switched to a black driver. In any of these cultural scenarios, some employees may just want information on what to do. Others may know how to respond, but they want your backing.

▶ *Find out what cultural encounters your employees are facing and how they are responding.*

We Want to Help You! (Organizational Cluelessness)

Suppose you had a group of customers who wanted to recruit more customers for you without charging you a dime. Would you ignore them?

Organizations *do* ignore these gift horses because they are just as unaware of culturally diverse customers as employees are in the Mystery Patient tours.

The demographic shifts in many parts of the country have still not been incorporated well in how businesses seek customers or how agencies and schools design their services.

The director of the Muslim foundation that hosted weekly gatherings of some 1,000 people implored our health care customer to give them information. "Women are constantly asking me for referrals because health care is so important," she said. "Give us information—we want to help you!"

Do you as a leader think of your customers generically and leave it at that? Is there room in the services or products you provide to think of your religious-based customers? Your gay and lesbian customers? Your customers who are deaf? Your military and non-military customers? One vice president in a defense company is trying to expand his managers' thinking that for years has been focused exclusively on serving a government customer. One of his managers is having trouble shifting his products to private applications simply because this is how he has always done things.

The possibilities are endless. If you fear that you might spread yourself too thin, remember that adaptations can be minimal. The Bank for White People was transformed in the eyes of the Latino consumer simply by having a bilingual employee. The Muslim group wanted brochures and information that already existed. Perhaps your focus on particular cultural groups would simply be to go talk to them. The reason the

Muslim women had no information from the hospitals was that no one had ever thought about it.

▶ *Think about it. Expand your idea of* *"customer."*

Do You Know Me? I'm Your Multicultural Customer

Some organizations *are* thinking about it. They're letting their information systems help them serve niche cultural markets and citizens.

One Community Affairs Office is using census data and school enrollments to identify population growth trends. They also pay attention to new businesses that reflect the influx of cultural groups. One new suburban business has let everyone know the strength of the local Latino population. The opening of Pollo Campero, a Guatemalan chicken restaurant, was met for weeks with constant lines that ran out of the restaurant around the outside of the store, at all hours of the day. Might make a business wonder: How can I serve Latinos, or how are they underserved?

Other businesses are coding their grievances and customer satisfaction surveys by language and ethnic groups to see if customer happiness differs by cultural group. Such surveys have prompted health care institutions in Los Angeles, Boston, New York and Virginia to establish clinics and obstetrical services for certain cultural groups and to provide advertising and educational materials targeted to them. Koreans in Virginia are thrilled that a Korean doctor connected to a large health care institution is regularly available. NYU Downtown Hospital's Chinese clinic has become so popular among the Chinese community that patients come not only from downtown New York City, but also from all the five boroughs. Patient traffic has built to the point of provoking expansion. The increase in customers has come primarily by word-of-mouth, confirming the research that demonstrates the unique marketing power of cultural networks.

Do you have information and systems that tell you who your customers are relative to the growing cultural markets?

▶ *Break out of customer cultural cluelessness. What cultural information do you have?*

Iowa and the Cultural Unknown

A health care institution didn't know that a Muslim foundation *wanted* to bring them more customers. A bank didn't know it was seen as a Bank for White People. I didn't know how to conduct an interview with a deaf man. Why don't we know these things about people who are different from us?

When I arrived to interview a branch head of a government agency who was deaf, it suddenly occurred to me on my way up the elevator that interviewing someone who couldn't hear me might be somewhat difficult. Now I was embarrassed. How was I going to do this?

There was nothing else to do but admit, "I don't know how to do this."

We often don't know about the needs, skills, even the desires of people who are different from us. We live in our own worlds, and we are often scared to cross over and look dumb.

Facing difference squarely is uncomfortable. Kids look at a person with a disability and pipe up, "That man has no arm!" Parents try to shush the kid. A friend stationed in Omaha who has traveled the world marvels that high school kids three miles from the Iowa border have never gone "over there" to Iowa. Their rationale? "Why should I? I've got everything I need over here."

If crossing over to Iowa is resisted, then crossing over to find out about customers who are black or Latino (and you're not), gay or lesbian (and you're not), deaf (and you're not), or who wear veils and have strict gender guidelines (and you don't) is likely to mean many people will not even consider it, much less make the move.

Yet when we do cross over in the workplace and in other situations, if we're backed by a few of the skills in this book, the experience is often surprisingly exhilarating. The person with no arm says, "It's OK. Let me explain," and he kneels down to talk to the child. The women with the veils have food prepared and are anxious to talk to you, since you have expressed an interest in their opinion.

The deaf man smiles and simply says: "No problem. Talk to me and don't look at the sign language interpreter, so I can see your lips."

Problem over, fear resolved. But it never would have happened if

- you didn't take the first step over the cultural line.

- you didn't say, "I don't know."

Before interviewing the Muslim women's group, I gulped when I asked the director on the phone, "Is there anything you would like me to be aware of regarding your culture and customs before I come?" She said, "Yes, please refrain from shaking our hands. I know it is common in this country, but it is something we women can't do."

Customers react well to people who don't assume things about them, who admit they don't know everything, and who are interested in their opinions. Culturally diverse customers with a history of being ignored seem to appreciate those things even more.

"Thanks for asking."

What is the extent of your outreach to the host of cultural groups—race, gender, age, religion, people with disabilities, people of a different sexual orientation, and so on? What, also, is the *quality* of your outreach? Are you and your employees skilled and honest enough to say, "I don't know your culture"?

By definition, for the most part, we don't know the preferences and experiences of those cultural groups to which we don't belong. Because of the often invisible barriers of fear and looking stupid, we frequently don't ask others' preferences or seek their business. Try it. It could be the start of a beautiful business relationship.

▶ **Have fun. Cross into the unknown . . . with the 7 Clues coming up next.**

PART TWO

Clues for Cracking
the Cultural Code

CLUE 1

LOOK TO YOUR ORGANIZATION'S CULTURAL GUIDELINES

No HARDENED VETERAN of corporate or government organizations would actually believe that one of those philosophical vision or values statements could help them with much of anything, much less how to manage the thorny issues raised by having different cultures in your workplace. So, this may come as a surprise: start with whatever your organization's diversity statement is.

A Cultural Lighthouse

One of my customer's expectations for cultural competence can be summed up in the following statement:

Cultural competence is a set of congruent behaviors, attitudes, policies, procedures, and services that enable XYZ to embrace *employee and customer cultural differences and customize our services to their needs.*

This statement is this customer's beacon for evaluating cross-cultural situations and deciding how to act. The word "embrace" is the crucial guidepost in this statement. As its leaders decide how to navigate culturally-related hazards, this organization is asking its employees to act in a way that *embraces* cultural difference, whether with co-workers or customers.

The statement does not say "tolerate." It says "embrace." Embrace is a strong word. It demonstrates how much the company wants to emphasize the importance of valuing differences in actions and decision making.

This does not mean you chuck all policies in favor of respecting differences; rather, the concept of embracing difference is a clue to keep in the forefront of your mind as you lead diverse employees and deal with diverse customers. The diversity statement becomes a practical tool.

In many cases, you may have to balance two seemingly competing interests. For example, in a hospital, an Indian family wants its whole family to stay overnight in the room with a sick relative. For safety and other reasons, you know that you cannot permit this; however, you do want to get across that you are respectful of this culture's family-oriented values. You decide to speak with the family leader about the hospital's policies, but you also add: "It seems very important for you to have family present with the patient. I simply need to reduce the numbers. How about if one of you stays overnight, and of course others can return during visiting hours?"

There are also many employee-employee situations where cultural differences are involved. Use your organization's principles for cultural diversity as a backup and guideline for handling these situations. Depending on the severity of the scenario, you might

- insist that employees embrace difference where behavior is very negative (say, team members not speaking to those different from them).

- counsel employees on what you would like to see from them in future cross-cultural situations. Give them a clear image ("embrace cultural difference" is one—you can choose another). They can then approach the situation with high-level guidance, and with flexibility to handle the specific details.

At Disney parks, the concept of the customer being a "guest" is a touchstone that guides employees in all their actions. In the same way, use your organization's cultural competence statement as a practical tool for addressing cross-cultural scenarios and problems.

▶ *Philosophy in action: a diversity statement.*

Why You Need the Platinum Rule

What if your organization doesn't have a statement of cultural competence principles? No problem. What you are after is simple guidance on how you want employees to deal with cultural differences. Whether the statement is created for your team or adopted organization-wide, whether it is written or regularly repeated verbally, the most important thing you will be doing is highlighting the importance of cultural diversity to your business, institution, or agency.

If you need some convincing about the importance of culture, keep reading this book. It focuses on the many ways in which we miss the influence of culture on customers and employees. For now, simply remember the value of giving high-level guidance to employees on expectations related to cultural difference.

Some readers may feel that general company principles related to customer satisfaction will fill the bill for guiding employees about cultural difference. My own experience says that is usually not the case. There is a great example of good customer service and lousy cultural attention in the chapter "Nice Doesn't Cut It," in part one on how customers see you. Many employees simply don't know what to do with the challenges presented by cultural differences. Others need skills.

For years, Southwest Airlines said that its employee manual consisted of one rule: the Golden Rule—treat others as you would like to be treated. Even this iconic prescription could be ineffective in a cross-cultural setting. As a manager, if you like being recognized publicly, would you publicly praise someone from a culture that is embarrassed by public praise? Would you use sports metaphors, because you love sports, to describe how to complete a task to an employee who knew nothing about sports?

Surprisingly, the answer to those two questions is often yes, because without attention to difference, many of us treat others as *we* want to be treated. A better option for the multicultural workplace is the Platinum Rule—treating others how *they* want to be treated. It would seem ridiculous to give a customer what we want instead of what they want, but it is done regularly in schools and hospitals and businesses because we haven't had our multicultural customers and employees on our radar screen.

So think of your principles of cultural competence as a way to attract diverse customers and loyal employees. What do you notice about your workforce, student population, or customers regarding differences, and what simple guidance do you want to give yourself and others on how to value difference? One small business owner noticed the difficulty in motivating workers of different age groups and ethnicities. Could it be that what motivates you and them differs by "cultural group"? Using our broader definition of culture that goes beyond race/ethnicity to include differences of age, region, and other distinctions, you may need a range of motivators for, say, different age groups.

▶ *Different strokes for different folks.*

Shed a Little Light

Use your experiences with diversity to tell your employees why culture is important to the business. Many organizations say simply that we value the differences among our employees and customers. Some use the word "respect." My customer went beyond this to say they "embrace" difference.

Some organizations include a rationale for attention to cultural diversity. They say that including culture in how one treats customers is a business imperative, given customer diversity. Or they state that a work environment supportive of cultural difference enables all employees to reach their potential and stimulates innovation, giving the enterprise a competitive edge. One company states that it wants to "encourage different kinds of thinking."

Here's what Merck says, given that every culture needs health care: "To succeed, we must bring together talented and committed people with diverse perspectives—people who can challenge one another's thinking, people who collectively approach problems from multiple points of view. We will continue, therefore, to cast the widest net in our search for talent—because it is the smart thing to do."[3]

Maybe your statement is as simple as "In a multicultural world, we treat employees and customers how they want to be treated." Whatever the verbiage, think about the importance of cultural differences to your organization's success, and craft a statement that will help your employees see what you want.

▶ *It's the 21st century. Give employees cultural guidance.*

CLUE 2

TURN TO THE LAW

THIS PRINCIPLE is straightforward: Be familiar with the primary laws governing cross-cultural interaction. As with Clue 1, laws can serve as a guideline to help you sort out specific situations.

Remember, though, that the laws don't exist just to enforce the literal requirements of government. The more day-to-day usefulness of laws is the *spirit* they are intended to communicate.

Get the Spirit

Think of the two primary categories of laws relating to culture in the workplace: antidiscrimination law and prevention of harassment. Essentially, anti-discrimination laws intend that everyone have equal access to work, positions, and success. Harassment laws exist so that no one should endure physical or emotional interference with their ability to do well at work.

The spirit that you want to create, therefore, as a manager, is that all of your employees can grow and bring their full talents and energy to their jobs. You develop everyone, including someone who speaks another language, has a physical impairment, or is older than other workers.

Many managers think they do this naturally. Many employees don't always agree. Give yourself a cultural checkup with the Clues that follow.

▶ *Combine your knowledge of the law with the spirit behind those laws.*

CLUE 3

CLARIFY YOUR CULTURAL LENS

THINK ABOUT THE THINGS PEOPLE do that annoy you the most: an employee showing up late, a person being rude or inconsiderate. Maybe you have a sibling or co-worker who can needle you about one of your traits that you'd most like to hide (my brother is a virtuoso at finding a soft spot). Very often, the things that others do that get us the most upset are actually the things we don't like about ourselves, or that we vow never to do or reveal. Psychologists call this "projection." We attribute our own feelings or attitudes to others—sometimes to those who display shortcomings we dislike in ourselves, or who activate our own fears.

Cultural Projectiles and You

Projection happens with cultural differences, too. If we had it drilled into us by our parents never to be late, then we may either stick to this rigorously, or drive ourselves nuts each time we are late. U.S. societal norms also have emphasized the importance of punctuality and deadlines. Given the vast number of people from other countries now living and working in the United States, we now encounter co-workers who have not grown up with the same time obsession.

That's where knowing your own culture and preferences comes in handy. If you know that you are a stickler about time, and you calmly accept that, then a conversation with a person who is not as time conscious will be on a much more even keel. If you see punctuality as a universal truth and not something that differs by culture, then your conversation with your employee is more likely to come off as blaming or as a put-down.

Apply this concept of knowing your own cultural preferences to many other differences—it is crucial for leading workforces of different races, languages, sexual orientations, religions, ages, physical abilities, and more.

▶ *Leader, know thyself culturally.*

Cultural Self-Honesty

Here are some common projections that arise in the United States simply from the cultural messages we get from media, our families, neighborhoods, or schools:

- whites being fearful of blacks, particularly black men, because of images of violence on the news

- Christians being suspicious of Muslims due to lack of exposure and understanding, heightened now by the aftermath of September 11, 2001

- English speakers being overly strident that English must be spoken in the workplace because "we're in America." No law says this; in fact, blanket, across-the-board insistence on "all English, all the time" could be against the law

To be effective cross-culturally, in the examples above, focus first on the fear, suspicion, or stridency. Notice what is going on emotionally for you in situations like these. Your feelings are the key to knowing what your cultural preferences are.

What might be some cultural sources of your reactions? Think about where you grew up and what the cultural messages were. Think not only of verbal messages, but who the role models were in your neighborhood and in the media. Think of the types of people you associated with then and now, by cultural difference. Have you chosen to live and socialize with people that look like those you manage and work with: gays/lesbians/bisexuals, other races, other religions, people with disabilities, and so on? Many of us don't, choosing familiarity over diversity because it is easier and more comfortable.

Noticing what you choose to do (rather than what you think) regarding other cultures will tell you a bit about what your cultural preferences are and where you may have some uneasiness. Be honest with yourself. One of the behaviors I believe we promote in U.S. culture is that no one should be fearful. Don't fall into a trap of denial because you don't want to admit fear. With cultural differences, there are always fears and hesitations about the unknown.

Your cultural background check on yourself prepares you for each cross-cultural situation. Say, for example, you are a white female supervisor of a group consisting mostly of women, and only one or two black men. You grew up in a largely white neighborhood, and you have an easy comfort with the white women on your team. If you review your own racial history, you may suddenly become more aware of the fact that the black men are more isolated on the team. Maybe they don't offer their opinions as much in the meetings, or they appear to be less comfortable with their co-workers than you.

In this instance, your knowledge of your culture and the gender and racial connection you have with the women allows you to think differently. You decide to simply become aware of what the effect of the large number of white women (of whom you

Cultural Lens

are one) is on the team. You may decide to step out of the comfort zone and engage the black men. Managers who do not know themselves well culturally might simply decide, "Well, I guess these men don't have anything to contribute." In turn, this thinking could wrongly affect your review of their performance.

▶ *Cultural upbringing and surroundings influence decisions.*

CLUE 4

APPLY
CROSS-CULTURAL
PATTERNS

JUST AS A HEALTH PROFESSIONAL can diagnose an illness by reviewing symptoms, so you as a manager can handle cross-cultural situations if you know what is going on. There are many cross-cultural patterns that are repeated over and over across the country. A few of them are:

Clueless Majorities

Insiders and Outsiders

Accumulated Impact

Intent versus Outcome

Denial

Just like seeing a familiar symptom of a disease, knowing cultural patterns gives you insight so you can resolve issues and be a positive force in cultural conflicts. You may be seen as a person who seems to understand all sides.

Five Patterns:
Crack the Cultural Code

Here are some key patterns and some suggestions on how to use them. I call them universal patterns because they can be applied to any cultural difference, be it race, gender, sexual orientation, language, religion, and so on. You can even apply these dynamics to the different organizational cultures that are brought together in a merger. There are Insider groups in a merger, and Outsider ones. There is denial, there are outcomes not intended, and so on.

▶ *Pull back from the problem—look for patterns.*

Clueless Majorities

A white male senior manager and a black female middle manager traveled to the Baltimore area to lead an all-hands meeting and hear employee concerns. Throughout the meeting, several employees referred to "Chocolate City." The white manager had no idea what they were talking about. (For all he knew, the city could have been Hershey, Pennsylvania, nearby home of the chocolate maker.) The black female knew exactly what the group was citing (Washington, D.C., with its majority black population).

The white manager's unfamiliarity with this term makes sense: if you are not a member of a particular group, you will be less familiar with its lingo, concerns, and way of seeing things. For example, I never knew what people with disabilities faced until my father ended up in a wheelchair on an oxygen tank. Double doors at hotels were a nightmare!

There are obvious downsides to cultural cluelessness: not knowing the needs of your customers, employees, or students. Or worse: turning off those groups unintentionally.

If you don't know and use the knowledge that majorities are often clueless, you lose the benefits that can accrue to your organization. You can turn knowledge of this clueless pattern into better cross-cultural relationships, sales, even strategies for inclusion of students or community members. Here's how.

Knowing that majorities are often blind to the needs of minority cultures, the first thing to do is to accept it. Don't try to fake that you understand someone else's experience that is different from yours. It's painfully embarrassing when you are exposed, and diverse employees trust you less. Be who you are culturally—even if it's clueless.

Know, also, that you simply will not be aware at times. Many heterosexuals put a picture of a loved one on a desk without thinking. Most are unaware that doing the same could be a daring act for a gay person, and that many gays, lesbians, and bisexuals put much emotional energy into whether to do so in their workplaces. In a "don't ask, don't tell" environment, displaying a picture of a same-sex partner would not even be possible. But if you're not gay, that problem is not likely to be on your radar screen.

Culturally effective leaders acknowledge that sometimes they will be unaware. In doing so publicly, they become much more accessible to diverse employees who need their manager to see the effect of cultural difference on their world. Looking externally, the same leader can use the knowledge of Clueless Majorities to ask, "Which cultural groups are we not talking to or seeking for business? Which groups are missing from our community meeting?"

Second, knowing that cultural cluelessness is natural, be alert to your organization's cultural numbers. Being aware that you may not know, for example, the effects of Christian references on Jewish people in your group (for example, referring to priests, ministers, churches, Christmas), you might ask them.

Alternatively, you might simply begin observing the majority and minority groups in your group on any important cultural dimension (religion, race, age, gender, national origin, language) to see if there are any dynamics you have been missing. Do the majorities give more input? Are you attributing performance weaknesses to individuals whose actions may have more to do with their being a member of an isolated group on your team?

I asked the lone black man in a group of all white women at a hospital what he thought of a just completed training session I conducted. He said it was fine, then added, "You know, I didn't feel I could be totally honest." He was outnumbered, and reluctant to put even more focus on himself because, I guessed, his colleagues "just wouldn't understand."

My own awareness of his quietness was because I knew the pattern of Clueless Majorities. I would wager that the women either didn't notice it, or, if they did, didn't have the skill or courage to recognize the pattern and invite his input.

> ▶ **Everyone can be clueless with culture.**
> **Use that knowledge to be more alert.**

Insiders and Outsiders

Left-handed people understand the concept of dominance, where the world is literally sized for right-handers. Our society is right-hand dominant, so right-handers set the agenda everywhere. Tools and desks are designed for right-handed people. People notice and comment if one is left-handed. And they devalue, sometimes without knowing it, the lefty. A friend who is left-handed had his mouse on the left side of his computer. A right-hander used his office and reported to him later, "Hey. I moved your mouse. It was on the wrong side." Stories abound about teachers who not so long ago forced left-handers to write right-handed, even hitting their knuckles with a ruler.

Similarly, in the United States, consider the following groups who are dominant, sometimes by numbers, but more important to this discussion, by power and position:

- heterosexuals

- men

- white people

- Christians

- people who hear

The importance of this concept when you are trying to create workplaces where everyone feels valued is that dominance can help those in the Insider group, and discourage those who are in the Outsider position. It is as if there are supportive cultural winds if you are a member of the Insider group in a society. Whites, for example, don't often think about being white in a majority white society—until they find themselves in a majority black neighborhood. Suddenly we are aware of our skin color and put some energy and thought into being self-conscious.

That self-consciousness is the frequent experience of anyone in an Outsider position. Gays and lesbians, bisexuals, people with disabilities, Muslims and Jews in the United States, and other groups often feel uneasiness, doubt, even fear. Add this knowledge to the way you manage people who are in both the Insider and Outsider positions in your workforce.

Here are some everyday ways you can take Insider/Outsider dynamics into account as you manage diverse people:

- Identify the Insider groups in your organization by diversity dimension (that is age, race, national origin, gender, sexual orientation, language spoken, position, educational background, and so on).

- Check if the opinions of Insider group members are holding greater sway in meetings. Women have complained for years that their ideas are ignored in meetings, or stolen and acknowledged as a man's idea.

- Be particularly alert to team members who are the only representative of their group on your team. Like the sole African American man in the training session I conducted, "onlys" may be more reluctant to give their ideas; they are even less likely to talk about the effect on them of being in the Outsider position.

- Seek opinions of the Outsiders if you feel they are holding back.

- As a way of giving yourself potential new insight, try tracking people's behavior by their *group*, not their personality. See what happens, particularly when comparing Insider and Outsider groups.

Add the skill of seeing cultural dominance to your repertoire. Cultural dominance affects the perceptions, interactions, and motivations of your diverse employees, customers, students, and constituents.

▶ *Make an Outsider an Insider . . . and grow your business, employees, and community.*

Accumulated Impact

There may be times when you run into an emotional buzz saw with someone different from you, and you don't quite understand why. You've just stumbled into history.

Accumulated Impact is the emotional load a person carries from long-time experiences of what a colleague, Chip Henderson, calls "micro-aggressions."[4] The end result can be that you say something you think is innocuous, yet the other person blows up at you.

Most of us can understand this, regardless of culture. You've had a bad day at work, you come home and your partner asks you to do "one more thing," and you explode. The partner wonders what she did to deserve this.

Bump this experience up to include cultural differences. You ask a woman or a member of an Outsider racial group who is new to your workforce to perform a task you consider a normal part of the job. The employee blows up at you, and you're surprised. You find out later that the employee feels she has consistently been assigned only low-level tasks and not given challenging, interesting work. She has experienced accumulated impact over time at the company, and you are now receiving the return volley.

Once you know about *Accumulated Impact,* here's what you can do:

Realize that occasionally you will trigger someone. If you notice someone react to you in a way that you find surprising and/or loaded emotionally, try first not to respond in kind. You might say, "Wow, it seems like I triggered something."

Ask. If you accept that you simply cannot understand the depth of experience or feeling of someone different from you culturally (remember *Clueless Majorities?*), then the logical action to take is to ask her about what you triggered, in order to get an understanding of the history you may have launched.

▶ **Check Accumulated Impact when "you just don't understand."**

Intent versus Outcome

Distinguish between these two, and your cross-cultural success will rise dramatically. When cultural differences exist, many things we *intend* are not received in the way we meant. Here is a classic example overheard at the coffee machine:

Chuck: *Laura, you girls did a great job on that project.*

Laura: *Uh, thanks Chuck, but please don't call me a girl.*

Chuck: *What do you mean?*

Laura: *You said "you girls" did a great job. I'm asking you not to call me a girl.*

Chuck: *I was just trying to give you a compliment.*

Laura: *I know. I would just prefer that you not call me a girl.*

Chuck: *I call my daughters girls all the time!*

Laura: *Yes, but I'm not your daughter, Chuck.*

Chuck's intention was to praise Laura. Unfortunately, his choice of words meant the compliment was lost for Laura, and the outcome was more connected to her history of wanting to be seen as a peer in the workplace. Chuck left upset with Laura and took the exchange as an insult—when his intentions were lofty! Guess what else? He did not include her on future projects.

Skill in managing different cultures requires the ability to separate out your intent from the impact your statement has on the other person. Muslim female patients have told of their horror when they are alone in a room and a male orderly enters. In their belief, it is a grave mistake for an unknown man to be in the room if another familiar male is not there with her. The outcome for the patient is devastating emotionally. The orderly may not even know he has had any impact.

Use the distinction between *intent* and *outcome* if you get a response to something you said that is contrary to your expectation. As a leader, you can often sort out cultural conflicts if you remember *Intent versus Outcome*. A manager had to counsel an African American male on her staff who repeatedly spoke with a Filipina co-worker in a narrow hallway with a raised voice, pointing at her close to her face. His intent was to get his "point" across. The woman was not taking in his discussion points. She was much more focused on feeling threatened by his finger pointing and the isolation of the hallway.

Interestingly, members of groups who are considered Insiders often focus on their *intention*. Outsider groups more often speak of *outcome* of a behavior or policy. This was the case for both Chuck and Laura and the African American–Filipina conversation. As a result, our cross-cultural conversations often become stalemates involving people trying to be right.

Watch for the *Intent versus Outcome* distinction in your employees' interactions. If a conflict between employees is chronic and stuck, try to get each person to understand intent and outcome. The manager working with the African American and Filipina co-workers could ask the man: "What is she saying the outcome is for her—what is she focusing on?" (It's best to start with supporting the person who is in the Outsider position first. His or her response is partly based on being discounted in the first place.) Once outcome is clarified, then the manager could ask the Filipina if she understands the African American's intent.

▶ **It's not who's right in a cultural impasse. Check intent and outcome.**

Denial

Try tracking news stories where racial bias has been cited. Invariably (I'm willing to bet it's 100 percent on this one), the organization's spokesperson will say, "This is not a racial issue."

OK, so maybe they have to protect themselves legally, but it would be refreshing to have the person simply say, "We're going to check it out," and leave it at that. As it is, you almost always hear denial of allegations of racial bias and it is easy to doubt the organization's credibility.

Consider, then, these variations on the denial theme in regard to other cultural groups:

- "This doesn't have anything to do with your being a woman. You're being too sensitive."

- "I don't have any problem with gays. I just don't want them to flaunt their lifestyle."

Perhaps a case can be made that in both of these examples the speaker is not in denial. But remember you are looking for ways to manage difference better, so you are concerned with how these comments are being received. How might a woman receive the first statement? If she hears that the speaker is so sure about *her* experience, she is likely to wonder, "How can he know my experience?" Furthermore, if the person is stating so strongly, "This doesn't have anything to do with . . . ," then maybe he really does have an issue related to her gender.

In the second example, the very word "flaunt" indicates that the person does have a problem with whatever the behavior is that she objects to as flaunting. So there apparently is some problem with some behavior of gay people, in the same statement where the person says she doesn't have a problem.

Denial is often rapid, mainly because many of us don't see ourselves as biased people at the core. The problem is that our denial also means we are not considering the other person's perspective. In the workplace, that leads diverse employees to mistrust their colleagues, leaders, or organization—just as we doubt the spokesperson who quickly denies a company's racial bias. For many years in our workplaces, as well as in society, cultural groups have said, "You're just not hearing us." Much of this reaction comes from Insider cultural groups automatically denying that race, gender, age, national origin, or any other cultural dimension could possibly have anything to do with a workplace situation.

Here are some things you can do virtually every day with the pattern called *Denial:*

- Slow down your response to someone who says that culture is involved.

- Ask the person to talk about how he sees the situation.

- Allow for the possibility that he could be right. You don't have to agree—simply hear how he views it. Go back to Clue 3: Clarify Your Cultural Lens and consider your own cultural upbringing. You might be influenced by cultural messages about which you are totally unaware. If the person is citing organizational policies and behaviors biased toward a group, clarify what the history and cultural composition of the *organization* has been.

A good example is a client organization whose demographic makeup is 80 percent white, male, and over 40. With that kind of predominance, it is worth listening to employees who are people of color, female, and under 40, to see if their experience in the organization is affected by their difference from the majority.

▶ *Denial is fast. Slow down with culture.*

The five patterns in Clue 4—*Clueless Majorities, Insiders and Outsiders, Accumulated Impact, Intent versus Outcome,* and *Denial*—give you a set of lenses to use in any cross-cultural situation, whether it involves race, language, education, two recently merged company cultures, disability, or any other cultural dimension. If you are stuck on how to resolve a cross-cultural situation, pull back from the problem as you see it. Look for these patterns. Then intervene by addressing the pattern: Are you dealing with the tendency to be clueless, or automatic denial, or accumulated impact, or what? The answer may allow a win-win for constituents who disagree on a policy, for employees in a conflict, or for customers complaining about your service.

CLUE 5

USE GROUP-LEVEL RADAR

MOST CULTURAL PUZZLERS are just that—puzzling. We are mystified by the "other's" behavior. Yet, you can add a new lens that will clear up a lot of mystery. You can significantly increase your cultural competence by adding cultural group radar to your repertoire.

Sometimes You're a Group

Consider that whenever you deal with anyone, you are not just talking person-to-person. You are working with people whose behavior and attitudes are *partly* due to personality. That's where most of us focus and try to fix things, or, more often, fix the other person!

When different cultures come into the mix, however, consider this possibility: you are now dealing with someone whose behavior and attitudes may also be influenced, say, by being Asian, male, Buddhist, even heterosexual.

The level of impact this may have on people's perspectives varies; here I am asking you simply to add this *group-level* consideration to your repertoire as a leader.

There are two sides to remember in regard to group-level impact: the actual behavior of the person, or the way they are *treated* as a member of a group.

For example, you may have some characteristics that you ascribe to being male or female—certain traits that you associate with your gender. In my case, my father taught me "boys don't cry." Other boys, coaches, and the mores of our society reinforced this lesson constantly; so, I see myself behave in accordance with that "law" sometimes, even though I think it's nonsense.

There are also times when I am treated as a group, not as the individual I am. When I jogged in my old neighborhood, I would pass women I didn't know. I would say hello. What was the response I got 90 percent of the time?

Nothing. No reply, and a look away.

Why? I presume this response had nothing to do with me at the *individual* level: Tom, the nice guy! Her response I am certain was a *group-level* response: in this case, I was MAN. That man jogging down the street might have been the Central Park rapist for all they knew, or a personification of all the media stories about men who attack women.

The important point here is that even if I don't believe I behave in ways that are associated with my "groups" (racial, gender, ethnic, sexual orientation), there are times when I am treated by others in accordance with *their view* of my group.

You can use this knowledge to improve your ability to work with other cultures. Try out the three everyday cultural strategies that follow.

▶ *Expand your repertoire—consider cultural group influence.*

Clarify Your Group Identities

Be willing to acknowledge that some of your behavior could be linked to your group membership. You just may not know it, particularly if you are surrounded by members of your own group. For one customer of mine, once one gets below the highest managerial levels, women dominate by numbers (if not always by power). Are the women aware of the impact of their numbers on the one or two men who hold positions in some of the units? I don't think they give it much thought.

Clue 3: Clarify Your Cultural Lens also comes into play in acknowledging group-level impact. Be willing to learn about your race, sexual orientation, family upbringing, national origin, gender, and so on, when you are managing people from all over the world. That learning consists of seeing how your group membership influences your preferences and decisions.

Here's an example of the influence of national origin on my decision making. While doing some consulting in Bolivia, I marveled that employees went home for lunch. When I mentioned this, several Bolivians asked me, "Well, what do you do?" I said I ate lunch at my desk. They said, "Well, when do you see your family then?"

Their question brought me up short about the value they placed on family, and how I was clearly giving work the priority over relationships. That priority I believe is fairly common in much of the United States. If I were managing these same Bolivians here, and they made their lunchtime a priority for staying in contact with friends or family, I am certainly aware of the possibility that I might judge them as less committed to their work, based on my own group's priorities.

The scenario is not too far-fetched. A Latino lawyer recalled that after sensing that his boss was not happy with him, he went to talk with him. The boss mentioned this very issue, wondering about the lawyer's commitment, after he returned from a long lunch with a customer. The lawyer felt that the firm's interests were best served by forming close social relationships with its clients; the boss put a higher value on doing hands-on work at his desk.

Who knows who was right? The point is to apply some insight to yourself culturally. Acknowledge where your cultural group background influences you, on several dimensions. Your employees may be experiencing the influence of your cultural preferences and you may not even know it!

▶ *Your cultural group membership is showing.*

A Third Way: Acknowledge Cultural Claims

You may object to the notion that your or others' behavior is related to group identity. Your cultural competence will be enhanced if you can hold off that objection, at least momentarily.

Leaders of diverse workforces with varied customers have to see cultural situations clearly in order to act with precision. Your radar gets fuzzy if you insert your own static, and handling cultural dilemmas gets harder.

Customers or employees may present a claim, for example, that their race is influencing their treatment or their opportunity. How do you resolve this?

In my experience, discussion of this claim usually goes like this: Whites may say other races are "playing the race card" to indicate that this group-related "card" is an excuse. At the same time, the other race doesn't believe the whites' denial, so the conversation goes nowhere, and the workplace situation festers. You as a leader in the group are caught in the middle. You need better radar.

Denial is one way of responding to cross-cultural conflicts. The other end of the continuum would be blind acceptance of the other person's explanation, or agreement because it would be politically correct.

I am suggesting a third way: acknowledge. Acknowledgment does not mean agreeing. You are simply holding off the impulse to deny while gaining an understanding of how the other person sees that, for example, their race may have influenced an outcome. As Dr. Delyte D. Frost writes in *Dialogue with Difference*,[5] you are "seeking" her point of view. You are actively curious, inquiring while staying open to that person's experience.

You're tuning in to culture, turning on the radar.

▶ ***Tune in to the other people's cultural experience—even if it's not yours.***

Sort

Sorting is the real "value-added" skill the culturally competent leader brings to a culturally diverse world. Most cultural logjams involve denial, such as the race card example. If you get past the impulse to deny, and acknowledge the possibility of group-related treatment, then you are including cultural factors in your set of facts for making a decision. *Sorting* means that now you can put *individual* factors next to *cultural* or *group* factors and evaluate situations with a bit more multicultural skill.

Let's say you are the manager of a security department, and a female Muslim employee thinks she was followed by one of your security guards in the parking garage. She comes to you later, after talking with members of her mosque, and says she felt threatened and under suspicion by one of your employees, and she is a fellow employee!

You know the guard and find him to be a warm person. At the individual level, you know him as a nice guy who would never do such a thing. When you ask him about it, he says he was just trying to ensure her safety by following her in his car through the parking lot to the entrance.

Should you tell her that she is wrong? If you stay at the individual level, you might, since you know your guy, and you believe he wouldn't lie to you.

In a multicultural world, *Sorting* means you need to go beyond the individual level. You add group considerations to how you respond, and then make your decision. Here are two possible conversations with the employee, the first staying at the individual level.

Alma: *I'd like to speak with you about an incident that occurred last week.*

You: *Thank you for coming, Alma. How can I help?*

Alma: *One of your employees in car 54 followed me through the parking lot.*

You: *I'm sure he didn't mean to follow you.*

Alma: *He did. All the way from my car to the entrance.*

You: *What are you suggesting?*

Alma: *I think he saw my head scarf and thought I was a threat—and I'm an employee!*

You: *Ma'am, I know this employee, and I'm sure he meant no harm.*

Alma: *He stayed behind me in the car the whole time. Never said a word.*

You: *I'm sure this had nothing to do with your being Muslim.*

Alma: *How can you be so sure? This kind of thing happens a lot.*

You: *Because we don't "profile" groups in this depart-
        ment. I also know the employee, and he would never
        do such a thing.*

In this example of a conversation staying at the individual level, you speak from knowledge of your
individual employee. Staying at this level also leads
to statements ("I'm sure this had nothing to do with
your being Muslim," and "he would never do such a
thing . . .") that imply you doubt her assertion about
the effect of her group membership. Even if you honestly doubt that assertion, there are ways to communicate, by using the skill of *Sorting*, that don't put her in
the position of being mistrusted, or you in the position
of being closed-minded, unhelpful, and even biased.

Here is the conversation when *Sorting* is added:

Alma: *I'd like to speak with you about an incident that oc-
        curred last week.*

You: *Thank you for coming, Alma. How can I help?*

Alma: *One of your employees in car 54 followed me
        through the parking lot.*

You: *You felt you were followed?*

Alma: *Yes, the car never left me, all the way from my car to
        the entrance, and I'm an employee.*

You: *Tell me how you were feeling at the time.*

Alma: *I felt threatened, and I felt suspected. I think he saw the head scarf and was suspicious because I am Muslim.*

You: *You were concerned that your identity as a Muslim raised my employee's suspicions.*

Alma: *Yes, absolutely. I have to admit, I was afraid to come to you, but I talked to members of my mosque, and they encouraged me to speak with you.*

You: *I am very glad you came. I definitely don't want you to fear talking to me, and I certainly don't want you to feel you are under suspicion at work. Have you had any other experiences like this?*

Alma: *I believe the September 11 attacks have made some people more wary of Muslims, and I do feel I am under greater suspicion at times.*

You: *I can understand why you might feel that way. I'd like to talk to my employee about your concerns. I don't want any of our employees feeling threatened. How can I get back to you?*

▶ *Managing diverse people means Sorting.*

Getting Framed

Thinking about the security guard, adding in the group-level consideration would mean this potentially jarring thought: Could the guard's behavior mean one thing to you, because you share at least his gender, and perhaps something different to a woman who is Muslim? Could the "nice guy" you know be more suspicious of this woman, particularly if the September 11 incident has influenced him regarding Muslims? (Understand, however, that September 11 is not the only reason here why an employee might act differently toward someone who is different culturally. It is very common for members of different cultural groups to experience the same person very differently. Some men I find to be great are not regarded as so great by good female friends of mine.)

Employees (and all of us) are often "getting framed"—perceived differently by different cultural groups. As a result, situations like this security scene get dropped into your managerial lap. What to do?

Use some of the cross-cultural patterns of Clue 4 (such as *Intent versus Outcome*) to have discussions with both parties, adding in the group level (see box below, *Sorting*). With the Muslim woman, you could start by focusing on the outcome as she experienced the situation, saying you certainly don't want your department furthering her feeling threatened. Your department's job is to make her feel safer, particularly since she is an employee. So you might ask her if there is any way the guard could have communicated that he was looking out for her. Or you could suggest that in the future you would ask your employees to make their intentions clearer.

In your conversation with the security guard, you would stress the group-level experience of the Muslim woman, and discuss with him how he could still accomplish his job of ensuring the employee's safety without scaring her. The discussion could also reveal to you what the employee might truly feel about Muslims. Here you also could engage the employee in an exchange to help him apply Clue 3: Clarify Your Cultural Lens.

Sorting

Individual-Level Factors	▶ Guard says he followed her like any other individual, for safety reasons. ▶ Guard is nice, in your eyes. ▶ You trust your guard; you don't know her
Group-Level Factors	▶ As a Muslim, woman feels suspected. ▶ Do you know how the guard deals with culturally different groups? ▶ Given the outcome for the woman, does your team need to adjust its methods, post 9/11?

The preceding table depicts factors in *Sorting* applied to the Muslim woman's concern. For another *Sorting* example related to gender, see "A Restaurant for Men?" in Clue 6.

In this example, you have sorted by including both the individual and group level in your consideration and actions. In other situations, *Sorting* may mean that you decide a scenario is more influenced by the individual-level dynamics than the group level, but you do not make that decision until you have done the *Sorting*, sincerely! Too often members of Insider groups in society are too quick to ascribe behavior or treatment to the individual's personality failings.

▶ *Unlock cultural disputes—Sort.*

CLUE 6

COACH PERFORMANCE CROSS-CULTURALLY

Your BUSINESS, AGENCY, OR SCHOOL can drive off cultural customers, as we talked about in the beginning of this book, without your even knowing it. The five Clues covered so far give you ways to see what outsiders see and to attract both diverse customers and employees.

Now let's begin to put those Clues into practice along with larger strategies for creating culturally competent workplaces. First, in Clue 6: Coach Performance Cross-Culturally, I'll provide some tips for managing individual employees who differ from you culturally. This Clue deals with your one-on-one management responsibilities of developing employees and managing performance. Clue 7 will focus on creating an environment conducive to inclusion, and part three will cover the use of all the Clues in common situations that leaders face.

Coaches with Culture

Coaching has moved beyond the sports world to the workplace. Just as a sports coach intends to improve the performance of individuals and a team, so too can leaders improve the effectiveness of their employees and organization by coaching employees to higher performance.

Coaching is an apt image for performance management. The idea is that the employee is center stage; you as the leader observe and provide guidance. Employees have a greater chance to grow if you are not doing it all. So let's use coaching as a stance or frame from which to do performance management effectively across cultures.

There are common themes to coaching someone well—whether as a sports coach or a performance coach. Some of them are:

- Know where you are going first. Clarify your own goals and philosophy.

- Be able to build trusting relationships.

- Have the person you are coaching (your coaching partner) develop "larger goals" connected to his life mission.

- Help the person clarify behaviors needed to attain those larger goals.

- Identify obstacles and comfort zones that keep him stuck.

- Be there to guide and provide feedback along the way.

- Integrate him with the team and the larger organizational mission.

- Believe in him and help him to be his best.

Think about that list. In order to do those things, you must have a strong relationship and credibility with the coaching partner. He must respect you to allow you to work with him in such a fashion, and both of you will need a great degree of openness.

Now let's throw into the mix that you and your coaching partner are from different races, countries, or religions, or that your team includes cliques by language or age, or that as a woman some men don't respect your authority as a supervisor. Or, as noted in the discussion of Clue 5, "sometimes you're a group" (others notice your cultural identity and act differently). And lastly, your coaching partner's experience may be affected by his gender, national origin, disability, and so on.

In other words, the coaching relationship is almost certainly influenced by cultural dynamics. A focus group of eight African American men felt if they were straightforward, because they were black, they were:

- labeled as "too radical"

- called arrogant

- impeded in their progress in the organization

- seen as complainers

All of these men were clear that culture influenced their ability to succeed. This means, as a coach, you need to work effectively with such perceptions. Some things that you have relied on before will still work. This chapter adds to your repertoire, updating your coaching for a multicultural workforce. How do you accomplish this already complex task of coaching performance when you must do it across cultures? The following chapters outline some guidelines for "cultural coaching," from challenging ingrained attitudes to overcoming performance blocks.

▶ *Coaching across culture is different. Add some multicultural depth to your skills.*

Before You Start

No matter what the coaching situation, you will be dealing with ingrained attitudes from the outset, some of which will be your own. Before you start coaching across cultural lines, clarify your commitment, credibility, and beliefs. You will improve your coaching dramatically.

Clarify Your Diversity Commitment

Define the overriding mission of your team, and the vision of how you want it to operate. That's the general management side that becomes a guidepost for making decisions on tough, everyday situations. If you have difficult choices, weigh them against this core purpose.

With a multicultural workforce, however, you need a guiding philosophy on cultural diversity. Clarify things such as:

Why is diversity important to you, the team, and the organization? Be very clear on this. If you're not sure why it is important, talk to people in the organization who do see the value. If you see attention to diversity as mere compliance, then your employees will too, and cultural difference won't serve your larger mission.

Most important, if you are coaching someone different from you, and you don't believe in the value of diversity, you may be indifferent to how your coaching partner experiences the world. Good coaches know the people they coach and don't dismiss their experience, but build from it.

How do the details of diversity relate to your important tasks? Clarify how diversity relates to recruiting, teamwork, future planning, and customers. Again, if you're not clear, ask your team, your customers, or the company's diversity representatives.

A study conducted in the fall of 2003 commissioned by America Online (AOL) regarding its own cultural competence showed why diversity was important.[6] A senior executive said: "We are going to die if we are not diverse. You can't run a business, a global business, with a roomful of white men. Particularly our type of business which operates in the mass consumer market."

Do you know why diversity is important to your team? Do you believe it in your bones, so much so that it shows up in how you coach across all differences?

▶ *Clarify your cultural diversity philosophy . . . and live it in your coaching.*

Build Cultural Credibility

Marie is an African American friend who went looking for houses with a white Realtor. In telling me about the experience, Marie said, "You know I had my radar on to see if she would treat me differently as a black woman, like asking me questions about how I could afford the houses." She related that she was working on her own natural reaction to situations like this. After a lifetime of different treatment, Marie knew she couldn't eliminate her radar, but she was working on acting the way she wanted to as a human being, regardless of how the Realtor treated her.

Her radar, however, is a great insight for leaders coaching across culture. You will be in your employee's cultural radar—whether they see you as a manager (different from their employee status), or different racially, by religion, language, sexual orientation, and so on. The radar may be highly tuned, if a person feels they have been mistreated often because of their culture, it may be dormant, or it may be more open.

There are three common mistakes managers make in the face of cultural radar that can ruin their credibility and keep them from being effective cross-cultural coaches:

They insist that the other person is being "too sensitive" about cultural issues. You can't know if this is true until you explore the issue. Don't start with this response—diverse people have heard similar comments from others for decades. You may just get lumped in with those others.

They feel uneasy coaching across race or other cultural dimensions because they think the other person is suspicious of them. They then act differently or may cut her more slack as a way of compensating. In the movie *Remember the Titans,* Denzel Washington catches his white assistant coach doing this by coddling one of the black players when he is tough with everyone else. The parallel in the workplace has been the complaint of African Americans for years that they often don't get honest feedback from white supervisors.

They make a point of telling the person they don't make judgments based on a cultural dimension, by saying, "I'm colorblind," or "I don't see you as black." A variant of this is trying to prove your cultural credentials: "I have a cousin who is gay and none of us have any problems with him."

Don't fall into these traps. There are alternatives in the next three sections that can build your credibility as an effective coach across cultures.

▶ *Credibility across culture: don't assume it. You've got to earn it.*

Face It: You Do Have Biases

People trust authenticity. It is a must-have for cultural competence.

It is impossible to grow up in this world without preferences and biases based on upbringing and the culture we grow up in. Most people accept that in theory. In practice, however, many of us don't translate that acceptance of bias into our behavior. We deny that our judgments are influenced by cultural preferences.

That denial can ruin your credibility with a person who is culturally different from you. I find there is something freeing about the calm acceptance that yes, I do have behaviors and attitudes that are group-based. My conversations across boundaries of race, religion, sexual orientation, gender, national origin, disability, and other dimensions are so much more open, relaxed, and successful when I admit to myself that I have bias. I'm not spending energy trying to hide something.

There are also times when I am hiding something, or I may not be aware of a bias and my counterpart is. Those are times when I am more jumpy and I become bottled up and ineffective.

Accept the fact that you do have attitudes, behaviors, and judgments that are related to the groups to which you belong. If you really believe this is true, then if someone from another culture brings up a behavior or attitude that is blocking your relationship, you are able to explore the comment as a possibility. The other

person can tune down their radar if they see you as honest. Your credibility will be enhanced.

▶ *Don't set off others' cultural radar. Accept bias, don't fight it.*

Admit Biases and Blind Spots

Nothing builds credibility and trust better than sincere admissions, and nothing can hurt respect more than denial or dismissal of cultural biases or blind spots. What person of another race will trust you to coach them on performance if you are quick to deny any mention that race could influence a situation? What person with a disability will ask you to mentor them if they see that you are uncomfortable with their disability?

When talking about sexual orientation issues in the workplace, for example, many customers will tell me,

"I have no problem with gays." In another situation, one manager said, "I worked my way up. I know what it is like for people at the bottom. I'm not so sure these other people do." I imagine the first reaction that gay people or "people at the bottom" would have to these statements is, "Uh-oh, he *does* have a problem." During the Watergate era, when Nixon said on television, "Your president is not a crook," the first reaction many people had was, "He's a crook!"

People can smell denial, so don't try to fake it. If you slow yourself down long enough to notice, you can feel the uneasiness and quickness in your response. You can sense your own "denial meter." Perhaps you are a woman coaching the one man in your group, and he has the courage to say that he feels his ideas are not heard in meetings. First consider yourself lucky that he told you. Then take advantage of this moment to strengthen the relationship. You might say, "Wow, I've missed that, but then again, I'm not a man. I'll try to tune into that. Tell me more about how you are seeing this."

You can do the same with race or language or other cultural dimensions. It is particularly important to admit where your vision and experience may be blinded about race, because managers as well as society are so quick to deny that race could be an issue.

▶ *Monitor your "denial meter."*

Do Your Own Learning

Another way to build cultural credibility is to focus on your own learning. Clue 3: Clarify Your Cultural Lens is the place to start to appreciate the influence of your cultural background and upbringing in order to work well across cultures. It is a must for establishing credibility in coaching diverse others.

It is not enough to say, "I'm a Heinz 57," as many people do when they speak about their ethnic background, to indicate that therefore they have no cultural background to investigate. View culture broadly—beyond ethnicity, language, and race—because each of us has been influenced in our preferences for behavior and attitude by all sorts of group affiliations.

When coaching someone different from you on any dimension, be clear about your own attitude and behavior preferences so that you don't impose those where they are inappropriate. I have had a fabulous coach for some time now whose personality is completely different from mine. She is detailed; I am big picture. She responds well to daily timelines; I seem to do better with larger, long-term goals and breaking projects up into chunks. The beauty of her coaching is that she helps me move toward accomplishment of my goals by helping me clarify ways of working that work for me. She separates out her way of doing things when coaching someone who does things differently.

You may have ways of success that are associated with your cultural group background. I notice, for example, that I have ways of dealing with conflict and solving problems that I consider very male, and some that I associate with how my family did things. As women, people of color, gays and lesbians, people from other countries, 20-somethings, and others take on more positions of power in a multicultural, global context, they will bring outlooks and behaviors to the workplace that are different from yours, but that work. Therefore, it's important to realize that your preferences are just that—preferences, not universal truths—if you are to be a credible coach across cultures.

Credibility in coaching multiculturally may therefore look less like

Try this. It works every time.

and more like

How are you seeing this situation?

(Wait for an answer.)

What are some of the ways you tend to approach situations like this?

Or

Yes, when I have encountered that, I tend to do this . . . based on my preference for. . . . What are some of your values and preferences for resolving conflicts like this?

This use of your knowledge of cultural preference is not only appropriate culturally. It builds self-confidence in the employees you coach because you acknowledge they have a valuable perspective to contribute. That distinguishes coaching from consulting and advice-giving; a coach should not be doing the work of both roles.

▶ **Build your coaching credibility. Know your cultural preferences and state them.**

"Oh, My God, You're a Completely Different Person!"

Building credibility, as we've just discussed, and clarifying your diversity commitment are two things to do before you start coaching cross-culturally. The last guideline before you start cross-cultural coaching can be summed up in one word: "believe."

Many leaders see managing culturally different people as a problem. Managers will tell me that too often people of color or women will "play the race or gender card" or use diversity as an excuse when, in the leader's eyes, this has "nothing to do with the situation." To be an effective coach, you must see your coaching partner's potential and positive traits. You've got to be able to emphasize the positive.

Positive belief is necessary because study after study shows that believing in a person's ability to accomplish a higher goal influences them to do great things. A classic movie example of this was *Stand and Deliver*, the true story of a high school math teacher in Los Angeles who believed in a group of Latino students on whom others had given up. Though the teacher had tough, high standards, the students excelled, influenced by the underlying, persistent belief of the teacher that they *could* master complex math.

To coach effectively across cultural difference, you have to have that underlying, persistent belief in your diverse employees. Inventory your beliefs. How do you really feel about each member of your multicultural workforce? If you have some negative views of their ability or willingness, it will show up in your communication and coaching.

Consider what your employees are involved in. They may be accomplishing things outside of work of which you are unaware, like raising a family, coaching kids, or leading a volunteer group. In a diversity training session I was facilitating, a black woman told the story of taking a work colleague to her church. The colleague was astounded at the change in this woman's behavior when she saw her in a new context: "Oh, my God, you're a completely different person in church. You're a leader, you're confident." The woman herself reported, "Here at work I come in and [she bows her head] just go to work."

People who are in support positions, or people who are from an Outsider cultural group in your organization, may be leaders in their own communities. You might miss this in the work context where they feel less honored and supported and more different.

You may also see epiphanies when the people you are coaching surprise you with a skill or idea. Consider how you can build your belief in their potential. You may need to "believe yourself" into believing in them, particularly if your perception is that they are using their culture as an excuse, by enlarging your view to include their lives, dreams, and skills that lie outside of work.

By attending to these first three aspects of coaching cross-culturally (clarifying the value of diversity, building credibility by being open about your own biases, and believing in your coaching partner), you have done important internal work, preparing the ground for an effective coaching relationship. If the relationship across cultural difference with your coaching partner is solid, you can move on to some classic coaching steps, enhanced with some cultural twists.

▶ *Believe. You may have completely different people in your midst.*

Jumping In

Since coaching in any venue (work, sports, dance) involves helping another person improve, workplace coaching must incorporate ways of moving a person beyond current mindsets and behaviors. So effective cross-cultural coaching involves bringing up bigger picture items, such as organizational goals, career aspirations, and performance gaps.

Cultivate Careers and Lives

Even when cultural difference is not involved, most managers don't take advantage of the tremendous motivational impact of working with an employee to develop her life, not just her job. The exceptions are notable. One restaurant manager I knew helped his employees make connections to *other jobs*, not because he wanted to get rid of them, but because he knew, for example, they were interested in computer careers. When this manager was moved up to a general manager position in another area, several employees appreciated him so much, they pleaded to go with him.

Language, religion, race and other differences often act as a subtle barrier to real dialogue between people.

This can block a manager from making a solid connection with an employee and undermine the performance coaching process. No one knew that the quiet, African American woman in that diversity training program was a significant leader outside of work. Start to sow the seeds for breakthrough performance by knowing where your employees would like to go—in their jobs and in their lives. Discover ways to meet their career ambitions with assignments, training, and rotations.

If a language barrier is blocking you from connecting to an employee's life goals, it's important to address that. Get an interpreter for developmental meetings, learn some words in his or her language—find a way.

▶ *Use life aspirations as a cross-cultural bridge.*

Develop Larger Goals

Setting goals may sound ordinary, but many people don't set goals in their lives or don't have experience in how to do it. The pace of the workplace today also promotes simply diving in, and discourages stepping back and thinking long-term.

Cultural differences, in some situations, can exacerbate the downside of not setting larger goals. Sometimes the leader-employee relationship is not conducive to goal setting either, particularly if you have not taken steps to establish trust and credibility. In some situations, particularly with employees who are recent immigrants, two things can happen:

- The manager may not initiate goal setting with workers at lower levels of the organization, perhaps because she doesn't think those workers want to advance. Or there may be a language barrier, or the manager may simply feel uncomfortable.

- The worker has never been asked to set goals and is unfamiliar with the concept of participating in his or her own development.

Ideally, the coaching partner sets the agenda for a coaching relationship. In a workplace setting, however, we are often talking about coaching in a performance management context, where the leader has responsibility for development. Though leaders may initiate the work, as coaches they can use techniques to get coaching partners to set the agenda. Perhaps the most important is to have coaching partners set their own goals, as this becomes their personal motivator for taking action.

Goal setting presents a golden motivational opportunity. Use goal setting as a chance to talk with coaching partners about their life goals, with the notion of connecting their jobs and personal development to those larger aspirations. If your employees are unfamiliar with the idea of setting life goals, you may want to introduce the idea to them in a group setting or in writing. Suggest that they think about life goals or come prepared to talk about them.

▶ *Think big. Think goals.*

Goal Tips

Setting goals need not be complicated. Start with simple conversation about where the person would like to go in their life and how this job can contribute. Be alert, however, to the things you can learn about what people are doing outside work that may show you a whole new side of your employee's capabilities and interests.

Goal setting has some standard components. Be aware, though, that cultural and personality differences may mean that your preference for certain aspects of goal setting may not motivate your culturally different coaching partner. Here are some of the standard components:

- Write out goals.

- Make them specific/measurable (things like what, when, how, by when).

- Establish both long- and short-term goals (so one can build toward the grand goal).

- List potential obstacles and ways to deal with them.

- Check progress and reward achievement; recognize milestones and accomplishments along the way.

Adapt these guidelines. Don't follow them to the letter if your coaching partner doesn't need everything written down or doesn't want to review goals as often as you. The point is to make a connection between the larger life goals and how your coaching partner might progress at work.

One way to adapt goals is to consider the purpose of goal setting. Here are some things that you are trying to build:

- Self-responsibility—the person taking charge of where they want to go

- Your knowledge—you want to know what their larger aspirations are

- Focus—goals activate us to see and do things that are related to what we are looking to accomplish (once you buy a Honda you see Hondas everywhere)

- Commitment—commitment spurs energy and activity

- Growth—the overall purpose of coaching is to help the person be the person he wants to be

If you are getting commitment, focus, and growth, and you know your coaching partner's aspirations, you can judge just how much of the "how-tos" above are needed. Some people may respond better to longer-term goals and not a lot of questioning about whether they have done something or not. Others may want more detail and more check-in with you.

▶ *Set goals, but be flexible in how it's done.*

Identify Improvement Gaps

Addressing perceived gaps in optimum performance will, naturally, first require you to have built up some cultural credibility (see the earlier chapter on credibility). Then there are some standard, familiar steps to follow in developing action plans for performance:

- Link the mission of the team or group to the individual. Given the team's goals, establish individual goals—that person's contribution to the team.

- Discuss that person's strengths in addition to gaps in their current performance.

- Plan action steps with the individual.

When you link your coaching partner's work with her life goals, you have enhanced these standard steps, as noted in the previous chapter. By including life goals, you demonstrate that you are more concerned for the whole person's progress, not just in getting particular tasks done. That is a coaching stance.

Let's assume you are skilled in the standard performance improvement steps listed above. What should you do differently when you are coaching someone from a different culture?

First, some things are not different. The organization and you as the manager have legitimate performance expectations so that the mission of the organization can be accomplished.

What you add is your knowledge of yourself and your radar regarding your employee and your organization. Identifying and working with performance gaps in a multicultural context is subject to bias like anything else—it's a matter of knowing yourself, or fooling yourself. As an effective leader across cultures, you must again be adept at *Sorting*, but this time it's in regard to whether the performance gap is real or whether you are seeing a gap that fits your preference or way of approaching things. Be careful here. It is easy to glibly say, "Of course it's performance," if you haven't built the earlier skill of knowing yourself.

▶ *Performance gap or cultural gap?*

A Restaurant for Men?

Here is an example of the *Sorting* process (see "Sort" under Clue 5: Use Group-Level Radar) you might adapt when you coach performance in a multicultural situation:

A female waiter at one of my customer's restaurants wanted to be promoted to "top gun"—a person who trained other waiters. She was told that if she weren't "so emotional," she could become a top gun. She felt this comment reflected a bias against her as a woman.

How would you approach the situation? Let's try *Sorting*. This time you would be sorting out possible organizational, group, and individual influences on the waiter's performance.

The restaurant is owned by two men and has as its branding strategy a desire to be perceived as a saloon, but with high-quality meals. Male and female waiters wear white shirts, suspenders, and ties. Top waiters become "top guns"—what could be a more male image as a symbol of success?

Several women have already complained that the culture is male-oriented. They say they feel excluded at times; at other times they feel they are expected to act in ways that are clearly male. So in this case

- the individual-level Sort is that this particular woman is seen as "too emotional."

- the group-level Sort is that women perceive a male culture that has a negative impact on them because they are different from the Insider group.

- the organizational Sort is the culture and its impact on how people are evaluated.

If you were coaching this waiter, would you consider her "too emotional" at the *individual* level? In other words, is she somehow using her emotions ineffectively, potentially impeding her promotion as a trainer? This could certainly be the case. This particular individual might need skills managing her emotions.

Sorting Influences on Performance in a Multicultural Situation
Evaluating a Female Waiter for a Training Job

Individual-Level Factors	▶ *Her personality is seen as "too emotional" for the job.*
Group-Level Factors	▶ *The manager evaluating her is male.* ▶ *There are no other female "top guns."*
Organizational-Level Factors	▶ *The restaurant's owners are both men.* ▶ *The dress for waiters is male: suspenders, ties, white button-down shirts.* ▶ *The restaurant positions itself as a saloon atmosphere—a "Cheers" with good food.*

On the other hand, you also need some agility as a sorter here. Maybe she is seen as "too emotional" because the whole culture is male (recall the cultural conditioning cited in the chapter "Sometimes You're a Group," that "boys don't cry"). The male manager's evaluation of her may be off-base because he is overlaying his preference and that of the male culture on how she is acting personally. (In fact, many performance evaluations of diverse employees focus on the personal rather than on performance.)

I am not advocating either position. I am saying that as a cross-cultural leader, you must be agile in your assessment: Is this perceived performance gap due to the individual's actions or to group or organizational influences?

Sorting is crucial to managing in a multicultural world. As a coach or manager, you are in the power position vis-à-vis the coaching partner. Your ability to be honest and open in performance assessment is not just admirable or character-building. It could make the difference in whether your employee grows, goes, or stagnates, and you could have a major effect on their self-perception.

If you decide in this case that the organizational and group cultures are influencing the evaluation of the female waiter negatively, your coaching of her will be greatly altered. You will have much more chance of success coaching her if she knows that you see the

cultural influences on her plight. You may not change the culture overnight, but a start with your coaching partner would be to work out strategies of how to swim in this "foreign" culture.

Sorting adds the cultural dimension to managing performance gaps. You maintain high standards, but you're not clueless.

▶ **Sort out the cultural gaps when you are identifying performance gaps.**

Six Ways to Overcome Performance Blocks

The real value of coaching is the promise of helping someone overcome ongoing personal obstacles and attain goals in life that he could not imagine. Coaching is most exciting and beneficial when the coach helps the coaching partner convert "I can't" to "I can."

To get to this level of depth and results, your relationship with any coaching partner must be open and direct. Your credibility as a coach, your trust in one another, and the ability of both parties to be open to feedback are key.

Establishing this level of relationship can present a problem in the cross-cultural situation. Human beings are often more trusting of and lend credibility to people who are like them, or who have gone through what they have. Good coaching across cultures has to break through the "he won't get it" barrier.

Many groups don't trust that the other person or group will understand their plight or needs. Take kids and parents, people of color and whites, women and men. Gays, lesbians, and bisexuals wonder how much they can say among heterosexuals. This social mistrust affects your individual workplace relationship with your employee.

The most common complaint in surveys I do with organizations comes from groups who are in a minority or Outsider position by numbers or power. They consistently say that they can't be open about diversity concerns for fear of retaliation, or simply because they feel the Insider groups in the organization will deny their issues or not understand them. One black male customer put it this way: "I don't say anything anymore. We're only authentic when we're home."

This is group-level mistrust. You may think this is unfair, because it may have little to do with you, the individual. But in cross-cultural coaching, whether you like it or not or whether you think it is fair doesn't matter. At the very least, group-

"Can we talk?"

level mistrust means you will be tested by your coaching partner, perhaps in subtle ways of which you are not aware.

It also may take some time for your coaching partner to trust you. On a team I once worked on, it took a year for a new member to trust that she could express her ideas—even though we championed participation—because her previous work experience had been one where she was expected only to work, not offer her ideas. It may not take that long for your coaching partner to develop enough trust for a productive relationship; the point is, cross-cultural managing often requires an added element of trust building.

So how do you get to the depth necessary for an effective cross-cultural coaching relationship, where personal obstacles can be openly discussed and great possibilities attained? Of course, the number-one quality needed in any relationship of such depth is mutual respect. What develops respect in a cross-cultural situation? Here are six ways of building respect cross-culturally.

▶ *To get past some performance blocks, chip away the cultural mistrust first.*

Beware Knee-Jerk Denial

You can't dismiss impediments that the coaching partner perceives come from being treated differently. You've got to see how she sees her world and her ability to progress.

Your first hurdle is the common tendency of majority groups to deny an Outsider group's experience. Denial of group experience ("she's playing the race card," "he's making excuses") is common because, if I am different culturally, it is hard for me to experience what others do since I am not in their shoes.

In cross-cultural coaching, if you are fortunate enough to have your coaching partner tell you about her different treatment based on language, gender, disability, and so on, don't blow it! *Your object is not to be right.* Your object is to understand her world.

Hold off your questioning of whether what you are hearing could be true. Instead, explore. Get your coaching partner to tell you how she is experiencing the situation. Suspend judgment; listen closely, and seek to understand.

Here's a typical cross-race dialogue where you're likely to lose your cultural credibility:

Partner: *That grilling was a little overdone if you ask me.*

You: *What do you mean?*

Partner: *I presented my plan for the finance system, and they jumped all over it.*

You: *It wasn't that bad.*

Partner: *Not that bad? I couldn't even get through the explanation of it for all the questions and second-guessing that was going on.*

You: *That happens to everyone.*

Partner: *I don't think so.*

You: *What do you mean?*

Partner: *They're obviously doubting me because I'm black.*

You: *That's not true. They just had questions they wanted answered. I've had the same experience.*

Partner: *I don't think you have.*

Taking this course, even if you're right, leads you to a new problem: your coaching partner now thinks you don't "get it." In the future, if there's something that legitimately involves his race, he's less likely to talk to you if you dismiss him on this one. As mentioned earlier, you don't have to blindly agree, but you could do something like this:

Partner: *That grilling was a little overdone if you ask me.*

You: *What do you mean?*

Partner: *I presented my plan for the finance system, and they jumped all over it.*

You: *And you felt it was overdone. I'm curious about that—how so?*

Partner: *Well, I felt I couldn't even get through explaining the plan. Every point was challenged.*

You: *And you felt something was odd or over the top about the challenging?*

Partner: *Yeah. After the fifth or sixth question, I started to think something else was going on here.*

You: *Tell me about the something else. What were you picking up?*

Partner: *This isn't easy to say, but I think they are doubting me more because I'm black.*

You: *Well, of course you know I haven't been in that position, but we know it happens. Are there tip offs for you? What was going on for you that gave you the feeling they were doubting you as a black man rather than the plan?*

Partner: *It was the continuous questioning. No acknowledgment of what would work, and continually picking it apart. And when I answered five or six questions, there was no statement of, "OK, that answers my question here." There was just more questioning.*

You: *I got it. Well, whatever their motives, it must drive you crazy to even wonder if that's the reason. I never have to think about that. Let's talk about how to handle getting this plan approved,*

> *which is your goal, and also how I can support*
> *you in dealing with your perception and the reac-*
> *tions of our folks. At the very least, I can start put-*
> *ting what you are saying on my radar.*

This second dialogue puts "seeking" into action. Just acknowledging his race by saying the words "black man" would be highly unusual, and effective, for a majority group member.

Also, remember that this is a cross-cultural situation. By definition, there will be some things "you just don't understand"; not all, but some. This does not mean that if the perception of being treated differently is one of the prime obstacles for your coaching partner that you will simply ignore it. It means that you and your coaching partner will have to work hard at the beginning of your relationship to know what those obstacles are so you can deal with them later.

▶ *Be a seeker, not a denier.*

Appreciate Cultural "I Can'ts"

Did you ever doubt your ability to do something because someone told you "you couldn't do it"? The cultural equivalent of this is called "internalized oppression." It means that because a group is treated differently, an individual member of that group begins to take in those messages and act according to the limiting assumptions placed on the group.

In most cases, the individual does not have to be told they can't do something. They internalize the group's doubts because they are able to see the writing on the wall. The classic case is people of color, women, people with disabilities, and other groups not aspiring to high positions in organizations because they see that no one at the top looks like them.

If you have never experienced being treated differently because of your group membership, don't be too quick to dismiss this dynamic. Coaching across difference is different. You have to try to understand and work with internal forces that have been reinforced day after day, year after year, to the person you are coaching—even though you may never have seen this dynamic or experienced it.

So be alert for the "I can't" assumptions or statements from your coaching partner that may relate to her status as "other" in your organization. Early on in the relationship, just "get it." Deciding if you should challenge the "I can't," and when, depends a lot on how you view the organization, as well as your partner. Your primary action here should be sorting the cultural or group experience from your coaching partner's individual performance hang-ups. Here's an example of the sorting (see Clue 5) you may have to do.

A common aspect of internalized oppression among culturally diverse groups is to have low or no expectations. One restaurant I consulted with asked me to interview employees on how much impact the company's empowerment program was having.

To interview the Latino workers whose job was to make salads, I had to go through the kitchen, then down some back stairs to a basement, a location that called up the word "dungeon." These employees never saw the customers. They had, not surprisingly, zero knowledge of the company's empowerment program, and no expectations for themselves other than having a job that was close to where they lived.

In cross-cultural coaching, your coaching partner's position in the organization, and the fact that there are few people like him outside the "dungeon" in positions of responsibility, can create a subtle but real obstacle precisely when you are trying to have your employee overcome obstacles. You have to be an excellent cultural sorter—there may be organizational sources for your employee's low expectations.

Don't miss the effects of the organization's structure and culture on your diverse employees. Internalized oppression exists. People may not want to admit it. Be alert to what roles diverse employees are in, where they are located, and the assignments they get. Catalogue the ways you see employees limiting themselves, particularly your coaching partner.

As a leader and coach, your job is to try to open up the possibilities of your coaching partner's world. Find ways to get your coaching partner to see beyond his circumstances. Even simple methods such as job rotation and increasing customer contact can challenge "I can't" assumptions.

▶ *Appreciate cultural self-limitation before you challenge it.*

Balance Reality with Challenge

So, you have not denied your coaching partner's potential group experience, and you understand that the experience of being treated differently may be limiting your coaching partner's horizons—what she believes she can do. How do you help your coaching partner move in the direction she and you want to go?

It is a tricky situation to be coaching someone when you may not have experienced what she has been through, and yet your work as a coach is to help that person move beyond her obstacles. You want her to get "unstuck," but it is not that simple.

Recall my African American friend's meeting with her white Realtor. Marie had come to a point in her life, after many years of being treated differently because of her race, of wanting to be completely herself, no matter what the potential actions of the Realtor would be. She was moving past her previous reaction of getting emotionally hooked, but, importantly, she was not denying her experiences.

There are clues here for you as a cross-cultural coach. First, my friend reached this point after years of negative treatment. You can't, as a coach, deal lightly with such history. You certainly can't provide "the 10 tips for moving beyond racism." Your credibility as a coach would be dashed. So balancing the reality of your employee's experience with the challenge of seeing new opportunities may take some time.

Second, Marie had goals, after being successful in many things, of wanting to be herself, despite the conditions. She clearly saw another way to be.

You may not be coaching a person who has done the introspection Marie did. Whatever the case, you have to respect your coaching partner's experience and move forward in skillful ways.

The first thing you can do is to believe in your coaching partner. See horizons for her that she may not. Essentially, the best thing you can do is hold an unshakeable belief in her that will influence how you coach at every moment. One way to demonstrate this belief is to envision greater responsibilities and opportunities for your coaching partner (see "Be a Developer" later in the book).

Next, work on her belief in herself. In a cross-cultural situation, this is where balancing reality with challenge comes in. You acknowledge the reality of differential treatment—and not in a perfunctory way. At the same time, you provide new challenges and opportunities. You help her see another way to be, but you do it by having her see for herself that she can do it through successes in the opportunities available.

Here's a real-life example: Dr. Edith Jones of Houston, Texas, was the first black woman to graduate from a major medical school some decades ago. She told me that she simply applied to the school, got accepted, and when she arrived, a shocked receptionist in one of the school's offices said, "But you can't go here." She simply ignored the clerk and said she had classes to go to and challenges to meet. She became a nationally known doctor.

Dr. Jones is an extraordinary person. Few people are like her; but her story is a good example for the cross-cultural coach. She acknowledged reality, but she didn't dwell on it. She used her vision of another place she wanted to be as a way of cutting through challenge. Your coaching partners will undoubtedly have a range of reactions that will differ from how Dr. Jones handled her first day at medical school. The principle for you to use as a coach, however, is to find that delicate balance between acknowledging and hearing reality and being able to help your coaching partner move forward.

Your timing will be crucial, and your sincerity is critical. If you have not experienced your coaching partner's cultural history, then your credibility in coaching will depend on your ability to hear her, not deny her, and understand as an Outsider. Whatever you do, don't take the "Oh, that's happened to me, too" tack and begin to relate your experiences. Effective cross-cultural coaching does not depend on your being like them; indeed if you "wannabe" like them and act that way, your credibility will be undermined.

▶ *Acknowledge cultural realities, but give the gift of your confidence, too.*

Use the Power of Patterns

Once I coached a basketball team. The best thing I could do for them was to see, from the sidelines, what they couldn't see. While they were in the middle of the action, I saw what all five of them were doing, and what the other team was doing. I saw openings they weren't aware of.

I also saw repeated patterns.

Noticing patterns in your coaching partner's attitudes and behaviors may be the best thing you can do as a coach. A coach can see actions in a different light. The shift in the way you see your coaching partner may just propel a whole new way of being.

My own coach saw one of my patterns. She noticed over time that I would report things I *hadn't* done since our last discussion, rather than what I had. This caused me to see that I did the same thing in talking about my day with my wife. So a pattern that surprised me (a positive person in my mind!) was the number of times I tended to focus on the negative. This led to several positive changes in the way I lead my life.

You as the coach can promote this kind of shift by looking for chronic patterns of words used, attitudes, actions, beliefs, interests, noninterests, and observations of your coaching partner.

One place to start is Clue 4: Apply Cross-Cultural Patterns (*Clueless Majorities, Insiders and Outsiders, Accumulated Impact, Intent versus Outcome,* and *Denial*). Using this framework, you may see that a blowup by your coaching partner was the result of accumulated impact, or that a conflict has a difference of intent and outcome at its core.

Even more artful and useful, however, is to track the patterns you see in your coaching partner's attitudes and behaviors. Listen to his words. Observe his actions over time. Hear how he reports what he thinks and does. Notice how his actions differ from his words. Collect examples of "I can't."

Then feed your observations back. Ask your coaching partner, "What patterns do you see?" The patterns you both identify give you indisputable data to work with. Your interpretation of that data could be disputable, but the simple reflecting of words or behaviors is effective coaching technique.

Use the patterns to identify, with your coaching partner, what the primary impediments are to his progress. Those obstacles will likely also show what exciting possibilities are blocked for that person.

Here is where knowledge of internalized oppression serves a useful purpose. Some of the employee's limitations may have a cultural source. You and your coaching partner may be able to unearth and discuss these cultural limitations. If they are out in the open, both of you can deal with them.

A good example comes from my own cultural background. In my extended family, which is primarily Irish-American, there is a tendency to not let people get too big for their britches. There seems to be a built-in "pretense meter" amongst us. If someone is fake or trying to build himself up too far, he'll get skewered.

I have now seen this family trait confirmed in a couple of books about Irish culture. The downside of this sometimes very funny "ability" to skewer, if you will, is that, if I take those words to heart, it may also limit me. Dreaming and thinking big, the source of accomplishment, may get cut down. Knowing this allows me to monitor that potential downer when I begin to dream big.

The key for you as the coach, coaching across cultures, is to get your coaching partner to see his own patterns. You can't presume to know the other person's culture—he needs to acknowledge his own cultural blocks. But as your relationship develops, you can jump start an employee's performance by reflecting back the patterns you see in what your coaching partner says and does.

▶ *Good cross-cultural leaders look for and reflect patterns.*

Use Your Radar

A customer was a very extroverted, big-picture guy. The coach backed off some detail he had to present and focused on the customer's larger goal for a project, sticking with the verbal exchange rather than written documents. Good coaches work with these differences. These are personality-driven, individual-level differences. They are not necessarily cultural in nature and are part of any good leadership development plan.

On the other hand, some differences between coach and coaching partner are cultural or group-related. It is not necessary that you know whether the source is cultural or not. You simply want your radar on in a multicultural world, focused to include cultural factors on your radar screen.

How can you activate your cultural radar? Start by using Clue 3: Clarify Your Cultural Lens. The more you know your own preferences, the more you can see others' cultural preferences. It's a paradox—to see others clearly, you need to know yourself clearly first.

Years ago, I trained people in Bolivia. I was leading a five-day program in the evening—a very public event. I prepared. At 6:00 P.M., I was ready.

No one was there. At 6:15, no one. At 6:30, a trickle. I was getting upset at this point. The program was timed out, and we were losing a lot of time! As people came in, my Bolivian hosts started serving drinks and hors d'oeuvres. We now had less than two hours to cover three hours of material. The following nights were the same, and I was going crazy.

Somewhere in the middle, my Bolivian colleagues told *me* to chill out. They said the participants were thrilled with the course, and that they had no problem going over the time limit.

I saw my clear preference for starting and ending on time. I never knew how strong it was until I left "Time Central" here in the United States, where we emphasize time so much. I saw that my time orientation was *cultural*, not a universal law.

My radar for the Bolivians was also clearer. They weren't late, bad participants. They were showing *their* cultural preference.

I became more calm and accepting, and a better trainer. As a coach, that same knowledge of your cultural self helps you see that your way is just that—*your* way—and you become more open to your culturally different coaching partner.

Of course some of "your way" will sometimes work for others. But if you tune in your cultural radar, you may see that some things that work for you need to be adjusted or discarded to work well with a coaching partner of a different gender, race, language, national origin, age, sexual orientation, and so forth.

▶ *Activate your cultural radar; direct it inside first, then outside.*

Match or Balance

A final method for developmental coaching that addresses getting employees past performance blocks is to "match" or "balance" the current state of your coaching partner. To match or balance cross-culturally, use Clue 5: Use Group-Level Radar.

If your coaching partner shares experiences related to her cultural group, and you explore those, you have more options open. You become more aware of culturally related struggles. You can then respond in a multitude of ways—empathizing, encouraging, even challenging—if you have held off denial.

There seems to be a range of how people react to negative culturally related treatment. Dr. Edith Jones marched right through it. Others use humor, others fight, others carry resentment, others oppress themselves, others rise to the challenge, others work to change the system. One person may have all these reactions. Indeed, many of my customers tell me they choose their battles—they simply don't have enough energy to fight them all.

What should you do as a coach when you encounter this whole range of reactions among the people you coach?

You need range, too.

You can use your knowledge of self as a first step to expanding your repertoire of coaching skills. For example, if you are a man who was conditioned not to show certain emotions, make yourself very conscious of that. In a coaching situation, you may need to show emotion. You may need to encourage, or express feeling in a sad situation. When you can introduce feeling or a new behavior, you are adding to your skill repertoire—in this case, expanding beyond your male conditioning. Most importantly, you are coaching appropriately to the cultural situation.

Sometimes you might match your coaching partner's feeling—laugh with her, or share her indignation. Other times, if you have a solid relationship, you might balance. This means you challenge your coaching partner's reactions if you feel she is oppressing herself as well as being oppressed. You might simply put your observation out: "This seems like internalized oppression—like you are doing as much of a number on yourself as they are on you! Let's form a strategy to move beyond this obstacle."

A keen sense of timing and a solid relationship are crucial to doing this kind of challenging—no tip can tell you when or when not to. Many people know this dilemma with their dear friends: sometimes it is best to support, and other times it is right to challenge.

Expand your cross-cultural repertoire. Develop skill using different emotions, attitudes, and behaviors.

▶ *Cross-cultural leaders need range.*

Be a Developer

Remember the salad makers in the dungeon? What if you thought of those salad makers in a different way? And what if you thought of your job as a leader as simply this: growing people?

With such an image, the salad makers would become mobile. Up the stairs they'd go to busboy, cook, waiter, maitre d', "top gun," supervisor, manager. Salad makers would be worthy of your attention.

There are a lot of culturally diverse "salad makers" (underappreciated, unnoticed people) in all parts of corporate America right now—in manufacturing, health care, retail—that I don't believe we in the majority groups are aware of. Many of them—surprise, surprise—have skills well beyond what they are doing for you. A local gym has a janitor from El Salvador who was a business trainer in his country. An Indian computer whiz works part-time selling clothes for a woman's retail store. A nearby Staples is employing a Latina phlebotomist while health care institutions are searching for them.

Being a developer in a cross-cultural world may take a little probing through the invisible barriers that separate us in the workplace, such as

Class (janitors are janitors, not trainers, in a class-conscious world)

Language (the reason I know about the trainer and the phlebotomist is that I speak their language)

Discomfort (cliques by race, language group, and national and ethnic groups are common among my customers, and many folks simply don't cross those lines)

Committing to developing people in a cross-cultural world involves a little more effort. Begin by crossing over the lines, but in the spirit of openness and curiosity.

"Tell me about yourself."

Make it fun. Do you enjoy hearing people's life stories? Ask them. Maybe learn some words of your workers' language (instead of banning it)! Be a little of who you were when you were a kid, when you didn't know what words like this meant:

- poor/well off
- white/black
- Latino/Native/Indian
- gay/lesbian/bisexual/transsexual

When I encourage you to be a developer, I am speaking of an attitude change, possibly a reframing of your job. Many managers see performance reviews as a great burden, but a senior African American manager told me that he spends a lot of time on performance reviews. He finds them extremely important because he frames his job as a grower of people.

His view is that employees want these conversations with their manager more than money or benefits, and they want feedback and development. His employees bear this out. One who had moved under another manager in a reorganization called him recently, saying, "Anthony, I want to come back!" Leaders who focus on developing people's lives, not just their jobs, are sought out. They are also great coaches.

▶ *Coaches are developers. Cross-cultural coaches cross cultural lines.*

Discovery: They Change, You Change

Cross-cultural coaching requires more humility than standard coaching. Inherent in a cross-cultural situation is the fact that you don't completely know the experience of "the other." Men don't truly know how women experience the workplace (and vice versa). The same lack of knowing applies to people with a physical impairment and those currently physically able; heterosexuals and gays, lesbians, bisexuals, transsexuals; whites and Latinos; support staff and top management (all the above with vice versas).

You are in for learning with cross-cultural coaching. As a leader of diverse people, you have to get over needing to be right or all-knowing. One of my managers hated surprises. It became almost comical to me to hear him react to any unexpected crisis saying, "I'm not surprised." To me, it was like a kid who wants to be seen as cool saying, "I knew that." He never wanted to be surprised because he wanted us all to know "he knew that."

Be surprised. If you look at a cross-cultural relationship as discovery and learning, you will get more respect from your coaching partner, and you will enjoy yourself more. The increased respect from the coaching partner will also open up your ability to challenge her farther down the road when necessary.

Here are some examples of responses that promote discovery, coupled with ones that are more likely to cause shutdown.

Partner: *There's no way I can move up the ladder here. They look at me in this wheelchair and say, "She's not leadership material."*

Coach: Shutdown response
That's not true. I made it. So can you.

Coach: Discovery response
Well, I can't say I've been in your position. What's this organization like for you?

■ ■ ■

Partner: *People think I'm stupid because of my foreign accent. In meetings people are speaking for me after I talk, saying, "What he means to say is. . . ."*

Coach: Shutdown response
Don't take it so personally. I'm sure they don't think you're stupid.

Coach: Discovery response
Ouch! How often do you get that? How do you feel and act as a result?

In the two cases above, not being disabled or as a native speaker, you need to see your coaching partner's world as clearly as you can. Seeing that world means getting things like advice giving and your experience out of the way. You are out to discover how he experiences your organization as someone different from the mainstream or the power players. You need that information to help him through two obstacles: the organization and his own attitude—the way he may be seeing himself.

Here are some of the benefits of using discovery:

- You have a more nuanced, accurate view of how the organization affects everybody, not just you.

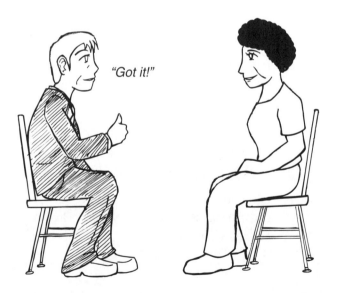

"Got it!"

- You are forced to articulate your observations and suggestions in a way that is more relevant to *another's* situation.

- You learn. You collect patterns of the impact of cultural difference. Your radar improves.

In sum, with discovery you become a more effective coach for people who are different. The word on the corporate street for leaders managing a diverse workforce is often, "He doesn't get it." If you include discovery for yourself as you coach, people will say, "He gets it. I can talk to him."

▶ *Be a cultural explorer, not an advice giver.*

CLUE 7

BUILD A CROSS-CULTURAL ENVIRONMENT

THIS BOOK IS FOCUSED MORE on everyday actions an individual leader can take than it is on organizational cultural change; but we do know that good performance depends on the effectiveness of the individual *plus* the environment in which he or she works. Your everyday cultural competence must be backed up by a foundation you help create: a workplace climate that supports cultural difference.

Environments for Diverse Employees

A multicultural world means not only that we have a multicultural workforce, but also that our customers are increasingly diverse. Clue 7 focuses on some things you can do to build a workplace where *employees* of multiple cultures thrive, as well as an organization that attracts *customers* of many backgrounds.

There are suggestions in many areas, such as information systems, structure, rewards, and organizational image. But they all correspond to a few employee and customer concerns, and one overriding desire.

Here are the primary concerns of diverse employees in the companies with whom I have consulted:

- Openness—the ability to be open about concerns related to diversity issues

- Optimism, not favoritism—confidence that they can progress and grow and that favoritism will not reign

- "Getting it"—the feeling that their concerns will be heard and not dismissed out-of-hand

What about customers? Of course they want a stellar product and good value; but beyond that, what do they want when you and your competitors offer similar quality and value? They want a sense that your product is their brand, your hospital is their hospital, your school is their school, or your restaurant is their restaurant.

In essence, diverse employees and customers want to belong. The following chapters describe some ways you can make that happen.

▶ ***Create an environment where multicultural employees and customers feel they belong.***

You Wouldn't Understand

Two employees won't go to their department head to raise concerns about her lack of support, response, and availability when they need her. One fumes, the other continually works around the problem, adding work to her day.

Standard advice here would be: "Use good feedback skills. Talk to the supervisor, and focus on her behavior and the impact on you."

Neither will do it. They say she gets too defensive and won't hear them.

Don't be like this boss when it comes to cultural issues! Her inability to hear concerns that involve her means she doesn't know what is going on.

Not knowing. The biggest chunk of cultural problems lies in not knowing what you don't know. It's like being in a foreign country and not knowing that you shouldn't bring white flowers (a symbol of death to some). This manager has created a workplace where employees won't raise concerns, so she doesn't know about the problems, extra work, and resentment she is creating.

Many organizations are like this manager. They often don't know how diverse employees see their climate. One of the baffling, frustrating reasons is this: Survey after survey in multiple organizations reveal that employees who are in an Outsider position by numbers or power (race, gender, age, sexual orientation, etc.) *will not tell you* how they are treated differently. They expect that if they were to tell you they would

- be labeled a troublemaker
- be called a whiner
- be seen as making excuses
- have the conversation turned around and be blamed

The effect is that you don't know the real deal about the environment you have, particularly as it relates to members of groups that are different from the company's mainstream demographic.

The first and best thing you can do to create an effective cross-cultural environment is to champion openness. Then any issue can be managed. But being

open on cultural issues, in my experience, is easier said than done.

How can you reverse the tendency of diverse employees to conceal their concerns?

Use Clue 3: Clarify Your Cultural Lens. Know what your preferences and hot buttons are. Accept that you have biases. When someone raises concerns about different treatment, relative to you or the organization, your self-honesty should make it easier to hear the person without first dismissing them.

Use Clue 4: Use Group-Level Radar. If you accept the general point that cultural groups can be treated differently, you are better able to entertain the possibility of someone's concern about different treatment. Again, you don't have to agree. You do have to be willing to explore, and do your sorting of whether this is a problem related to the individual or to the way the cultural group may be treated in your organization.

A group of engineers in a regional branch of a national company grew tired of repeated rejections of their ideas by headquarters' engineers. They were told to stop whining and follow HQ's method. Were they whiners, or was this a group-level pattern called "Headquarters versus Region"?

Whatever the answer, these three young engineers began circulating resumes, concluding that the environment did not support difference. This company is losing the current "war for talent" by encouraging highly-sought engineers to leave. A leader who is a good cultural Sorter would easily nip this problem in the bud by turning on his radar to employees who feel like Outsiders to HQ.

Be Alert—Track. Use a skill called *"Tracking.*™"[7] Follow, *by cultural group,* behaviors like participation or the lack of it in your group or the organization. Track the number of culturally diverse managers, the kinds of people you hire, even the people you tend to socialize and party with.

Do you favor, for example, certain people in your organization? That's natural. Usually we attribute this to individual factors, like personality—we like this person more than another.

As a multicultural manager, add this skill to your repertoire: Track who your favorites are by cultural group (age, gender, sexual orientation, race, language, religion). Be assured that even if you don't track, your employees are tracking. I recall as a young man that my company continually put the same people—usually older—on exciting projects. I began to think certain people—by their affiliation as older, white men—were favored. That kind of wondering is going on everywhere.

When you do that kind of tracking, you can short-circuit the wondering. If you notice cultural favoritism, group members will feel freer to bring it up, particularly if you don't sanction them. Be comfortable with *Tracking*, and they will be comfortable talking about their culturally related concerns.

▶ **Track cultural behavior. There will always be cultural information "you just don't understand."**

Looking Up Gets Me Down

You want employees to be optimistic that their organization is a place where they can thrive and progress. If you have employees who speak languages other than English, who have a disability, who are gay/lesbian/bisexual, who are people of color, or who in some way don't reflect the top of your organization culturally, stop and think about optimism and motivation.

As a white man, I am amazed at the difference the profile of the higher ups, or the people who seem to get the rewards, makes to those who don't look like that profile. My amazement is tied to the fact that I don't have the experience of looking up and seeing that my race and gender might mean my journey will be harder. Twelve percent of all corporate board members in the U.S. Fortune 500 at this writing are women, even though more than 50 percent of the population is female. One percent of those board members are black women. This is not an attack on men or white men—these are just facts.

The implications in your workplace, however, are likely greater than you think. Many times I have heard comments like this one following a speech championing diversity by the CEO of a global financial company: "He says he's for diversity, but I don't see a lot of people other than white men sitting up there with him on the management team."

We know that children do as their parents *do*, not as they *say*, so why would companies, schools, and agencies be any different?

The demotivating effects of not seeing diversity as you go up in an organization are legion: "Will I ever have a chance here?" "How could they ever understand that women (men), people of color, young people (older people), nonmilitary (military) people are not favored here? They haven't lived my experience!"

The flip side—the motivating effects of seeing diverse people in responsible positions—is also possible. I see this often when I team up with black women to lead diversity training and consulting efforts. During breaks, black women in the participant group will often gravitate to my partners. There seems to be a natural desire to talk with someone in authority that at least knows your story and won't dismiss it.

▶ *Cultural role models motivate.*

Playing Favorites

It's impossible to reflect all of your employees—you're only one person. What can you do as a manager to make sure looking up isn't dragging down your people's performance, or resulting in effort that contains little excitement and commitment to the organization?

First, don't dismiss this reality. Many of you might say, "Everybody can make it. If they let the company profile stop them, it's an excuse for not performing. Look at Colin Powell—he made it."

Consider that this view may be how *you* are seeing cultural difference dynamics. If your employee doesn't see it this way, whose view is he going to act on, yours or his own? It may be that you don't want the employee to give up before he starts, but, particularly if you are not a member of his culture, it is likely that he will simply dismiss you as not understanding his reality if you dismiss him.

First, in order to build a strong cross-cultural workplace, find out if being different from your organization's hierarchy is a block for members of your team. You may not be able to change the larger organization right away, but you want to get a sense if there is a business case for diversity in this regard; that is, is there an effect on your employees' motivation, regard for, and commitment to your organization? Goldman Sachs and Scotiabank realized they had miniscule numbers of female partners and senior officers. Both launched initiatives to address the disconnection women felt from senior levels.[8]

Second, and even more within your control: Do an honest assessment of yourself and your own organization culturally. So much is unconscious with culture there is no need to blame yourself for anything. Simply begin to look at what you do. Track by cultural group and consider:

To whom do you give the major responsibilities? Most people track this at the individual level; that is, they tend to lean on those who they feel are responsible *individuals* over time. So you may see yourself as simply going to people you feel are "go to" people.

Try pushing the cultural *Sorting* process. When you think of those to whom you give the most important assignments, what people, by race or gender or age group or language or ability, get the assignments?

Do you favor any cultural groups? Simply become more conscious of the little things—going to lunch, following up certain employees' comments and not others' in meetings, listening better to one group than another. Try it: do a mental scan of the people you meet with most often, go to lunch with, listen to, or seek out. Then check for yourself: do these folks belong to particular cultural groups? As a leader, you need to be more conscious of your actions, so are you sending any unintended cultural messages by virtue of who gets your attention?

You dismiss *Tracking* by group at your own peril, because your purpose is not to find out who is right about favoritism, but whether your *employees* are tracking cultural favoritism. Normally, people who are different in some way from the larger culture will be more alert to *Tracking* than the mainstream (recall the pattern of *Clueless Majorities* cited in Clue 4: Apply Cross-Cultural Patterns).

Many people believe they are blind to cultural differences and fair, not playing favorites with one culture or another. I am urging greater openness here because with culture, it is more common to not know what you don't know. It's like the classic fish story: the fish never knows that it is swimming in water until it is out of the water. If we grow up in one culture, we do things we don't even think about. It becomes essential, therefore, to see beyond your own "water" when you are a multicultural manager.

▶ *Employees are tracking cultural favoritism. Are you?*

"Getting It"

There are certain experiences I will never go through and therefore never completely understand. For instance, I'll never be pregnant. I'll never fully "get" all the lifelong implications of pregnancy for the mother.

Similarly, in managing cultural differences, there will be many experiences you will never fully get about how your employees who are different from you experience the world and your organization.

The importance of "getting it" to create a climate where difference can thrive, however, is not to make you identify with the other person. Indeed trying to do so can be comical and offensive, and worsen the climate. I cringed for the thousandth time at the eye doctor's office one day when I heard a middle-aged white man overdoing his attempt to identify with the young black man assisting him by saying, "Thanks, man" a couple of times. One of the things I appreciated about my father being "square," as we used to say, is that he didn't try to be like us teenagers.

You can get it without losing yourself. The idea is not to identify, but rather to hear their perception, not dismiss it.

The history of diversity in the workplace is that the victim gets blamed. Sexual harassment is the classic case of this, where those who are harassed are much more often reluctant to say anything because they feel the spotlight will fall on them for being overly sensitive or provocative. And though whites feel blacks "play the race card" too often, many blacks actually play it very little, because they don't want to be seen as making excuses.

"Getting it" simply means that you and your organization are willing to acknowledge that different treatment is possible—even if you don't agree that there's a problem. So you use Clue 3: Clarify Your Cultural Lens and Clue 4: Apply Cross-Cultural Patterns to acknowledge that bias exists and that group-related experiences happen. Just remember it's not easy. When I am told I have done something that indicates a bias, my first reaction is to defend.

All of "getting it" about the impact of culture, however, does not have to be reactive. You can create a climate that champions diversity through modeling—an active demonstration that you know in your bones that competence with different cultures helps your business. Do you, for example:

Talk with your employees about how cultural difference is affecting the sale of your product or service, the evaluations your teachers do of students, or the new ideas you are getting from your team?

Talk about cultural competence at all? Is it ever an agenda item in meetings, a consideration in strategic planning, or part of a product plan?

Make personnel moves that show your belief in the benefit of diversity by knowing the hidden talents of your employees, having a diverse management team, including people from outside your team for input at a retreat or planning meeting?

Factor diversity into your customer approach by using a diverse team to present to the customer or distinguishing how customers receive your service by cultural group?

Evaluate the impact of your workplace climate on different group members? For example, do men experience your organization differently than women? I was struck, for the umpteenth time, in doing focus groups at a university, how white men saw little impact of diversity on performance, perception, promotability, and climate. In the next hour, eight African American men, given the same questions, not only had clear examples for every question, but agreed that they experienced similar obstacles in many different departments and levels.

Use opportunities to fill open positions by at least having a diverse pool of candidates? Diverse employees have told me many times that they watch the pattern of how openings get filled, and they are often disappointed that the same people by cultural group fill those places. Are you tracking this?

▶ *Demonstrate "getting it."*

Mortar Between the Bricks

Up to this point in Clue 7, the focus has been on intrapersonal and interpersonal attitudes and behaviors that you can employ to build a productive environment for diverse employees, such as *Tracking, Sorting,* and role modeling.

Now we will address some organizational and managerial actions you can take to build a culture that demonstrates that it values cultural difference. These attitudes, mechanisms, and organizational changes add up to sending a message about cultural difference and its significance to the business.

Permeate, Don't Legislate

Making anything, including cultural competence, a program in an organization is the kiss of death, the first step toward marginalizing it. You can't make cultural competence a training program and figure, "OK, I've covered cultural diversity!" You also can't make it a law, or make it an EEO or Affirmative Action thing. Then it becomes an onerous requirement.

For cultural competence to be beneficial to your customers and your business, it has to be alive in everyone's minds and connected to the crucial tasks of your organization.

The connection of cultural competence to the business starts with you, the leader. Clue 6: Coach Performance Cross-Culturally stresses that you must first sincerely see and believe that cultural difference affects your business. If you see the connection clearly, that will begin to influence others. The first step to having cultural competence permeate your organization is your own modeling.

Organizations reflect their leaders. This is a maxim you can take to the bank. Consider this example: A division's managers seem to have trouble confronting employees. No surprise. The division director doesn't like conflict.

You can do the reverse. You can create a workplace environment that champions cultural competence by modeling cultural skills yourself. Here are some suggestions:

Speak about it.   Talk with employees about the business case for diversity. Describe how your customer base is changing. Observe and report how diversity of perspectives contributed to the success of a project. Make clear what your expectations are regarding diversity; for example, including cultural breakdowns in analyses or future plans, or having a diverse pool of employee candidates.

Act.   With whom do you spend your time, by different cultural dimensions? Consider expanding with whom you go to lunch, give responsibilities, and so forth. Notice cultural differences, and do the kind of *Tracking* and *Sorting* discussed previously.

Show.   Demonstrate that you value the importance of cultural diversity by follow-up actions. Because a CEO met monthly with various community groups seeking feedback on his organization's services to those groups, one employee who served those groups said she was extremely aware of her performance to those culturally diverse customers.

▶ *Create a workplace culture; be the atmosphere you want to see.*

Reward Cultural Competence

Two teams have equal sales numbers. Would you reward the team whose sales reached more diverse markets? Would a teacher be rewarded for making the curriculum more multicultural in focus? Would you reward a manager for assembling a diverse team, figuring you'll get more creative solutions and services?

Behavioral science tells the story on promoting certain behaviors: consequences drive behavior. If you want certain behaviors to continue, then reinforce them positively.

If you have been a leader very long, you already know about consequences in the area of general management. For our purposes, we are simply moving the principle of consequences toward encouraging certain behaviors and discouraging others in the area of cultural competence.

Consider this example: One organization that has championed cultural competence for years tried many approaches. One key player said: "We tried food and ethnic festivals. We tried training. Nothing really worked until we put expectations for cultural competence into the performance appraisal system."

When employees knew they could be rewarded or punished for attention to cultural diversity or lack thereof, the workplace culture changed.

In addition to modeling cultural competence, then, you build an environment that supports culturally different employees and customers by ensuring that cultural competence gets reinforced. Check first your performance appraisal system and your own evaluation of employee performance.

Do you have expectations related to cultural competence for your employees? If you yourself see the link between cultural skills and your mission, then you will have task-related needs for cultural sensitivity included in job descriptions and expectations.

Do your marketers and salespeople analyze cultural segments, grow the business by engaging different niches, and devise strategies that include cultural factors? Do customer service people deal equally well across the spectrum of your customers, or do they complain about or mock people with accents from other regions? Do your managers and employees have difficulties working across language, race, gender, physical disability, sexual orientation, or other groups?

One of the keys to encouraging the culturally sensitive behaviors you want and discouraging what you don't is to have performance expectations in the area of cultural competence that have an impact on people's jobs and rewards. Before you set expectations, clarifying the connection of culture to job may be the extra support that you as the leader have to provide.

Many employees and managers I work with claim not to see the connection of diversity to their jobs. You can help employees make this connection, but remember one of the universal cross-cultural patterns discussed in Clue 4, *Clueless Majorities*. In my experience, those who have trouble seeing the connection are people who don't experience different treatment by culture (read: those who are in the majority or who are Insiders in society or in your organization).

This is where your clarity on the importance of cultural competence becomes necessary. If you are unclear about the connection of culture to your business, get the help of your employees and customers who *do* see the connection. Many times the most convincing diversity-related examples are co-workers' stories of the treatment they get related to their culture.

▶ **Reward cultural competence. Connect culture to the job.**

Discourage . . . Carefully

The area of rewards also includes the need to discourage behaviors you don't want. Here you may use "punishment" (the performer gets something he doesn't want, such as reprimands, not being promoted, or discipline) or "extinguishing" a behavior (the performer does something and nothing happens, for example you ignore or don't build on particular comments).[9]

Be careful about rewarding and punishing. Rewarding and punishing in the area of cultural competence requires skill in the technique of cultural *Sorting* as described in Clue 5: Use Group-Level Radar. You will need to distinguish different people's interpretations of motivation and behavior because they may be reacting from their own cultural biases.

Language cliques are a good example where *Sorting* will be necessary. If cliques keep team members apart, or block information flow, or even cause people to refuse to help those outside their clique, then these are behaviors you want to stop because they are affecting the accomplishment of your mission.

There are times, however, when the person who feels excluded because he or she doesn't understand the language is creating a problem that is bigger than the reality. Many times people who speak another language are not intending to exclude others at all. They are simply enjoying the opportunity to relax. Have you ever gone through the taxing process of speaking a language other than your native tongue all day? It's exhausting.

So you may need to work with the person who feels excluded before you punish a group speaking their native language. If the job is getting done and people are still able to work together effectively, the problem may not be the foreign language speakers, but

rather how the one feeling excluded is taking being the Outsider. Many people who are normally in the majority—in this case, English speakers—have never had the experience of being in the minority. That experience may be just the thing this person needs in order to deal with your customers who are regularly Outsiders.

▶ *Before you punish, Sort.*

"Skill Up"

When we survey diverse people about their organization's effectiveness with diversity, one of the top three inhibitors in the workplace culture is always their perception of barriers to opportunity. Create an organizational culture where diverse people progress. A recent news report quoted a Congressman saying, "As people with disabilities, stop giving us pats on the head. Give us a job."

Motivational studies for years have shown that increasing responsibility is one of the prime motivators. If people in your organization know they can move up or do new things, you add another brick of credibility to your workplace foundation of managing cultural diversity effectively.

Start by taking on the attitude of "skilling up."[10] Skilling up means finding ways to utilize current employees in new roles and responsibilities by adding to their skill base. This attitude and technique has profound advantages when applied to managing a multicultural workforce.

Here's an example: A large organization in the Los Angeles area, one of our nation's most culturally diverse regions, continually recruited telephone operators from outside the company. The traditional pool of prospective telephone operators was made up of white women. They already had the operator skills, but not the skills needed to deal with an increasingly diverse customer base of varying ethnicities, languages, and socioeconomic classes.

The organization already had a diverse workforce that matched these customers, but they did not have telephone operator skills. The company's diversity coordinator pushed for skilling up. His notion was this: It would be easier to teach the technical and customer skills of working the phones to the company's current diverse employees than to teach cultural competence skills to new employees who might not have the connection to the company's diverse client base. The company's current employees had that connection.

Skilling up can be done with blue collar or professional employees. Many organizations around the country have immigrant workforces in some of their lower-skilled jobs. (Latest census statistics showed 12 percent of the country being foreign-born, with greatest concentrations in the West, South, and Northeast. And those populations are significantly younger than the native-born population, meaning greater concentration of the foreign-born in working age groups.)

Yet the immigrant workforce is only one part of the employee population that could help organizations through skilling up. Many of these employees are people of color, people pigeonholed by the department they work in, or people with disabilities who are limited by an employer's blindness to their potential.

Do a review of how you have doled out responsibility and promotions over time by cultural group. Consider several cultural dimensions: national origin, language spoken, gender, race, sexual orientation, region, military versus civilian.

If you are spreading the wealth, great. If you see yourself through your actions (not necessarily your beliefs) picking the same cultural groups for top roles or positions, review your thought process when you made the selections. Can you start adding skilling up to your management repertoire? If you hear yourself saying, "Isn't he a little young?" or "She's good technically, but I'm not sure she's management material," try to make your fear of risk realistic. Could you skill up with a person who is different from your company's mainstream, and thereby make a statement that will have the larger effect of making your business more culturally competent?

Skilling up offers three advantages to your organization:

- You create a culture where current employees see opportunity.

- You expand your pool of potential candidates.

- You reduce recruiting costs.

▶ *Build steps for everybody in your organization. Skill up.*

Do You Know Me? I'm Your Multicultural Employee

We have information on most everything now. Companies know their customer's likes and dislikes. Computer cookies give Amazon and everybody else a read on the fact you bought a Bruce Springsteen CD, and the next time you're online, poof! Would you like Bruce T-shirts, a book about Bruce, or CDs of artists similar to Bruce? With the Internet, the sky's the limit on how much information you can get.

The amazing thing in managing diverse people is that managers and organizations often lack the close-to-home information about the full range of talents their own people can offer.

Keep in mind the example of the African American woman who served as a leader at her church but whose talent went under management's radar at work. The organization only found out what it was missing because a fellow employee happened to go to church with her and saw her leadership experience in action.

What's more, people are not the only ones who are missing information on the talents their fellow workers have to offer. Information systems are often inadequate because organizations have not keyed in important cultural information. For example, a large health care

system with several hospitals had 580 doctors from other countries on its staff. When checking their information system, 340 of the 580 entries had *no* information on what other languages these doctors spoke.

Information on languages spoken could be crucial to this organization. It sits in a large, metropolitan area with numerous immigrant populations, many of whom have good incomes and networks within their ethnic group. A number of customers now search hospital websites trying to find out if their language is spoken there.

What's a manager of culturally diverse employees to do? Ask yourself, do you really know them? To what hidden talents and experiences might you be blind, and do your information systems give you any insight?

The reason we overlook these things in business is that we don't consider them important to the task at hand. So in upgrading your information on cultural factors on your people, go back to your beliefs about cultural diversity. Do you believe that attention to your diverse employees and customers will enhance your business?

If your answer is yes, then talk to your employees to expand your notion of their skills. Ensure that your information systems provide relevant cultural data. A simple way to start is to inventory all the languages spoken by your employees and the interests and skills they have.

▶ **With your diverse employees, look deeper.**
With your information systems, get cultural.

Structure: Who's Where?

One employee in a defense company looked up and saw all former generals at the top. Limits the possibilities, wouldn't you say, for all us nongenerals? What would, say, a person with a disability look up and see in your organization?

Stop for a second and look at your organization from the standpoint of your employees who are in some way different from the mainstream. Track, by different cultural dimensions, who are in the top positions and who get the major project responsibilities.

Track culturally, how many of your top managers have an obvious disability. How many are women, how many are men? How are they distributed by age group? Look at, for example, who leads the "power departments" by race or other dimensions, and who leads support departments.

What would diverse people see, either in the total organization, or in your part of the organization?

To be sure, representation is not everything. EEO departments have been concerned about this for years. Cultural competence is more holistic and relates to how cultural diversity can contribute to your business.

Taking a cultural look is worth it because your employees are looking. Even more jarring: your customers are increasingly taking the same look. One major manufacturing company in the South told me it lost a significant contract because its customer saw more diversity in a competitor's organization. If you see a predominance of one group, then addressing the structure in some way may be important to the motivation of your employees, and could even win you some business.

Making change in the larger organization, depending on your position, may require a longer view. Some things you can do now in your own organization:

- Talk about what you see, and consider with other managers what it means for the business.

- "Skill up" your own diverse employees.

- Require diverse pools of candidates for jobs.

- Pay attention to how you dole out responsibilities and check if you are unconsciously or subconsciously missing people.

- Expand your knowledge of your employees beyond your assumptions.

▶ **Take a cultural picture of your organization. Your diverse workforce already has.**

Expect Cultural Affinity

"**M**ost of my friends are white. I am white. And it is kind of who you know when you are hiring somebody. And it is hard to break that circle of friends. It is a leap. It is the reality."[11]

This quote from an AOL employee speaks to the more subtle nature of what managers are up against if you need good cross-cultural relationships for teams to produce superior products and services. Most of us lean toward comfort and ease, and with diversity involved, that comfort is often with someone who understands your background, your language, or what you experience.

In contrast to subtle preference, some of you may face the more pointed obstacles to teaming that prompt my customers to call me: cliques based on language or national origin that seem to exclude others, race problems, or even fights.

Whether subtle or extreme, you can't legislate relationships. To some extent, people are always going to gravitate toward those with whom they are naturally comfortable.

There's no escaping, however, that most teams and departments have to work across differences now. The workplace is, surprisingly, the place where a minor revolution in cross-cultural relationships has to take place, because many of our residential neighborhoods—where we go home at night—are still heavily segregated by culture.

So what can you do to get the relationships you need for the business to thrive—without forcing cross-cultural teaming down people's throats? Here are some ideas to try:

You can set the environment and the expectation for cultural partnering. If you have followed Clue 7's suggestions so far on setting the workplace foundation for cultural competence, you have

- permeated the organization with a commitment to cultural competence because you have repeatedly made the case that diversity contributes to your business.

- rewarded cultural competence and commitment by providing positive consequences for it, and negative repercussions when cultural exclusivity interferes with the business.

- created opportunity for diverse people by skilling up.

- made cultural information part of what informs your business.

- expanded your knowledge of your diverse employees' talents and experiences.

Without trying to force specific relationships cross-culturally, you have made the work environment conducive to cultural competence by having people talk the talk and walk the walk. It is harder to sustain exclusive behavior if inclusion is "in."

You can model relating across cultures. If you are crossing cultural and departmental lines, your employees will do it, too.

You can accept "natural affinity." Don't fight the fact that people connect along cultural lines. You might be surprised how many of my customers actually fight affinity. One potential customer called me concerned that "blacks are gathering at the water cooler." When I asked what diversity issues the organization had, he said, "That's it."

Reacting against such gatherings furthers the separation I believe people fear in these "water cooler" cases when cultural groups meet. If people connecting on some dimension of their cultural background are truly interfering with the business, you can talk with them calmly about how to meet your business needs while leaving them the freedom to speak their language, for example. (It might be a challenge for you, however, to truly find a business reason if you are honest about your own biases.)

Remember, you want *all* of your employees' talents, ideas, and perspectives to be brought to the challenges of your business. That is your larger goal. So you don't want to cut off the parts that make up the core of who they are as a person.

You can use your workplace advantage: the binding power of a task. Since the workplace is the location where different cultures are getting together, you might as well take advantage of the basic driver to bring people together at work: the task. You can promote the practice of relating across cultures by giving diverse people a common task. Here you can be a little more forceful about the need to relate across differences because you are responsible to the business for getting that task done. We've had cross-functional tasks and teams. Why not cross-cultural ones?

▶ *For cross-cultural relationships, go with the flow . . . and open the spigot a little, too.*

Keep Them Coming Back

There is an old customer service statistic that applies to the head nods you get when you ask, "Was everything all right?" Nine out of ten customers won't give you the feedback that something was wrong. They'll just never come back.

With diverse customers, the probability of not coming back likely increases if the problem is caused by poor treatment related to one's group. One professional woman hasn't been to an Acura dealership since a salesman opened up an Acura trunk and said to her, "And you'll like this for shopping because the trunk is so big!" She hates to shop. She hated the assumption he made even more.

So how do you prevent your customers from dropping you, the extent of which you may not know? You can start by using some of the lessons covered with employees:

Don't react with denial.   Many people who nod and never come back because of group-related treatment won't bring up an incident because they figure you will deny it, and that you just won't understand.

Use Clue 5: Use Group-Level Radar.   First, accept that sometimes people do get treated differently because of their group. You'll be much calmer when you have to react. Second, remember you *want* their view— they're your customers.

Train employees to accept group-level impact.   At the very least, school them about the pattern of *Accumulated Impact*. If they can't accept they may have bias, they can perhaps accept that they could trigger someone's history of discriminatory treatment. It takes good emotional skill to realize this and then to work with the customer on acknowledging his reaction and making things right. Teach this.

▶ *Teach cultural reaction skills.*
  Keep customers.

Polish Your Points of Contact

Go beyond reacting. Be proactive to attract and keep diverse customers. How good is your cultural customer contact?

Check out head nods. In retail, this can mean going beyond saying, "Was everything all right?" and following up the question.

"I wonder what our diverse customers think of this place."

Those who follow up in the diversity area either have had a similar experience themselves, or have developed their radar and skills. So, first check your "cultural contact" by seeing if your organization reflects the diversity of your customer base.

That reflection could be a multitude of things:

- the diversity of the team you present

- the relationships you build (do your employees cross cultural lines, or do they gravitate to those like them?)

- the product or service you produce (should diversity be incorporated?)

Even if you don't totally match your customers' diversity, employees can use skills (such as the 7 Clues) to check out head nods. For example, in a school setting, principals and teachers should directly address cultural difference with parents—proactively, before the parents bring it up. Ask them if they have needs and concerns related to diversity. One school system is considering how it will address the growth of ethnic and class differences in a population that was formerly all white, middle- and upper-class girls. All the above actions can be termed "seeking" (see Clue 5: Use Group-Level Radar, applied to diverse customers).

Prevent head nods.   Finally, in addition to reacting well and seeking well, how about proactively generating enthusiasm among diverse customers? Think about the myriad points of contact your customers have with your business: telephone operators, phone calls, pictures on the walls, all manner of interactions, promotional material, the teams that interact with customers. Consider your business hours. Do they match the needs of potential customers with diverse backgrounds—working parents, different religious groups?

Harry Beckwith, in his great books on marketing,[12] urges making each of these points of contact extraordinary for any customers. Add culture to that idea. Start thinking about making points of contact extraordinary for the cultural groups that make up your growing demographic sectors. A defense company, for example, has a prayer room for Muslim employees and visiting customers from Muslim countries.

You are looking for ways to bring in and keep those customers who either are not daring to enter yet or who are trying you out. Make your points of contact culturally creative. Do the pictures of your board of directors on the wall add to the positive experience of your new and rising clientele? Or do those pictures cause your prospective customers to think this isn't a place for them?

▶ *Shock and attract diverse customers. Use creative cultural "points of contact."*

Tip Sheet: Cross-Cultural Environment Building

You can attract multicultural customers and diverse employees by using the suggestions in Clue 7 to send a message about the importance of diversity to your business. I've suggested these ways to influence workplace receptivity to diversity:

- *Tracking* by cultural groups—who gets assignments, who is at the top, with whom do you spend time?

- Permeating—being the cultural role model you want to see in the organization

- Rewarding inclusive behavior and discouraging its opposite

- Structuring—seeing where diverse people are in your organization, and what role diverse customers play

- Using natural cultural affinities and providing cross-cultural tasks

- Expanding information systems to include cultural data

- Enhancing your image to customers through "seeking" and points of contact

You can influence your team, department, division, or organization through these individual inclusive actions and attract many new customer niches through the face you show to the market. Reinforce that image with a diverse workforce that feels it belongs.

Setting up an inclusive environment will have an enormous positive impact on the common dilemmas that follow in the next section. All of them should be much easier to solve (and may not occur at all) if you have prepared the ground by making fulfilled diverse customers and employees a driver in your business.

PART THREE

Opportunities
to Turn Clueless
to Competent

*The 7 Clues graphic shown at the bottom
of the left-hand pages in this section
reminds you of all the Clues.*

Before You Start

This part brings to light some common cross-cultural scenarios that today's leaders and organizations face. To give you guidelines for handling each situation, I suggest the Clues that best apply to each scenario. You may see some themes from earlier in the book repeated in the solutions to the situations. That's the idea: the power of the Clues and fundamental patterns described in parts one and two is that you can combine and apply them in different ways to address a wide range of cross-cultural issues in the workplace.

Multiply Your Options

When leaders are stuck regarding any problem, they often see their options as limited. They may say, "It's either this or that," or "We've tried everything," or "I have no idea what to do." When you are facing some cultural dilemma in your place of work, I would encourage you to use more than one Clue when considering what to do. Multiply your options.

By understanding the 7 Clues, you are familiar with the basic tools for being skillful across cultures. In short, that means that for each cultural conundrum you encounter, you can bring:

Clue 1: Look to Your Organization's Cultural Guidelines

Using your organization's principles for diversity as a guide for decision making in cultural situations. One customer's guiding words were "embracing difference."

THE **7 CLUES**	1. COMPANY GUIDELINES 2. LAW 3. YOUR LENS
	4. CULTURAL PATTERNS 5. GROUP RADAR
	6. COACH 7. ENVIRONMENT

Clue 2: Turn to the Law
Basic knowledge of the laws governing cultural competence. In essence, that means preventing harassment and discrimination. But remember the intent of the laws: to provide opportunity and growth for everyone in the workplace.

Clue 3: Clarify Your Cultural Lens
Deep understanding of your cultural background and preferences, so that you can see how your cultural upbringing influences your judgment of the current situation, and whether you are going overboard on your preference by making it universal law.

Clue 4: Apply Cross-Cultural Patterns
Understanding some principal patterns of cross-cultural dynamics, such as *Clueless Majorities, Insiders and Outsiders, Accumulated Impact, Intent versus Outcome,* and *Denial.*

Clue 5: Use Group-Level Radar
Your new lens for taking group-related influences into account when assessing a culturally related situation.

Your options for solving cultural problems are increased further if you manage performance well cross-culturally, and establish an inclusive environment. Clues 6 and 7 suggest some ways to do both.

Clue 6: Coach Performance Cross-Culturally

Your coaching attitude (looking for ways to support employees) and skills (authenticity, openness, and connection to larger goals and values, such as embracing difference).

Clue 7: Build a Cross-Cultural Environment

The foundation you construct through information systems, structure, rewards, relationships, and organizational image.

▶ *Ease cross-cultural situations. Bring all your tools.*

Check Your "Be" Before You Do

As you apply the 7 Clues to particular situations, think first how you enter any cross-cultural situation. Here are two different modes of entry reflecting philosophies about diversity.

THE **CLUES**   1. COMPANY GUIDELINES   2. LAW   3. YOUR LENS
4. CULTURAL PATTERNS   5. GROUP RADAR
6. COACH   7. ENVIRONMENT

Many people fear that focusing on difference creates problems. In my opinion, if you see diversity as a problem, it will show up as a problem—a self-fulfilling prophecy.

Others focus on what can be achieved by capitalizing on and even emphasizing the differences before them. They start with a fascination with difference that expects new, creative ways to solve problems and create business opportunities by people "differentiating"— maintaining and growing people into their uniqueness.

If you are calm and enjoy differentiation, you can enter cross-cultural situations with confidence in your ideas and openness to more than one possible solution. The positive way to enter is a way of *being*, not *doing*. This way of being more than likely makes 95 percent of the difference in the success of whatever you do.

I'm saying you can influence whether you have diversity "problems" by your attitude toward diversity.

So as you think about the following scenarios and your own situations, review how you might "be" as you enter the situation. What is on your attitudinal "packing list"? What is your first reaction when you read the scenario? Is your reaction in line with your organization's principles? Are you overreacting? Can you see ways to make difference an advantage in the situation, rather than a liability?

Your grand entrance when intervening will be grand not because you just got dressed up, but because you've learned about yourself, cross-cultural patterns,

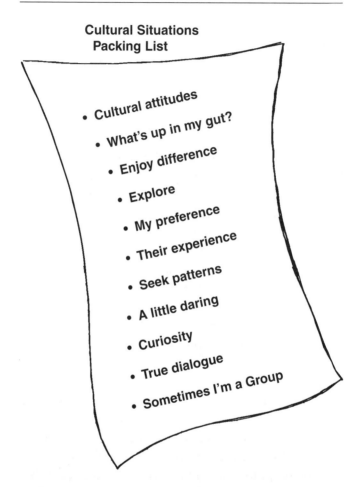

**Cultural Situations
Packing List**

- Cultural attitudes
- What's up in my gut?
- Enjoy difference
- Explore
- My preference
- Their experience
- Seek patterns
- A little daring
- Curiosity
- True dialogue
- Sometimes I'm a Group

and group-level dynamics—and because you've practiced a little and put yourself in cross-cultural situations. As a result, you have decided how you want to "be" with diversity: embracing of difference (instead of denying), open about your own biases, and informed about how groups function.

▶ *Enjoy difference when you manage difference. Your attitude will make the difference.*

Ten Familiar Scenarios

From here we look at ten specific cross-cultural situations that are common in the workplace today, applying the 7 Clues and emphasizing those that seem to fit particular situations best. The situations posed are

- Customer-employee relations
- Cultural cliques (by language, race, national origin, and so on)
- Employee-employee relationships
- Glass ceilings and favoritism
- "You're in America. Speak English."
- Political correctness
- Reluctance of minority groups to be open
- Joking (about sexual orientation and other diversity dimensions)

- Majority members insisting, "I'm not prejudiced. My parents raised me to be colorblind."

- Cultural conflicts about conflict

You may have to adapt your response to your workplace and its culture. Rather than follow these suggestions to the T, try to understand how the 7 Clues are used. That way you can get the benefit of the principles and still apply them appropriately to your own situation.

THE 7 CLUES	1. COMPANY GUIDELINES 2. LAW 3. YOUR LENS
	4. CULTURAL PATTERNS 5. GROUP RADAR
	6. COACH 7. ENVIRONMENT

Customer-Employee Relations

Generally, in managing a cross-cultural problem between a customer and an employee, work the problem so that you don't lose the customer *or* the employee. The goal is to end up with something mutually acceptable and beneficial.

Sometimes, however, you may *want* to lose the customer or the employee.

Here are some common customer-employee situations with suggestions on using the 7 Clues.

Discriminating Against the Customer

Companies such as Denny's and Eddie Bauer once were in the news as subjects of suits and complaints alleging past discrimination against African American customers. This repeated discrimination is the most extreme example of mistreating culturally diverse customers. Two of the 7 Clues apply to preventing this type of cross-cultural problem.

Clue 2: Turn to the Law

Train employees on the laws against discrimination, and lay out the consequences for them as well as for the company if those laws are violated. Remind them of the spirit of the law and its benefit for the company:

Why would any business want to drive away customers?

Clue 4: Apply Cross-Cultural Patterns

Train your employees about the notion of *Accumulated Impact*. Remember the "radar" my black colleague turned on before meeting a new Realtor? (See "Build Cultural Credibility" under Clue 6.) To a greater or lesser extent, depending on the person, many members of diverse cultural groups are alert to the treatment your employees give them and recognize biased treatment. They may even mistake some behaviors or attitudes as culturally biased because of their experience of *Accumulated Impact* or mistreatment by others.

If you expand the definition of culture as this book does, customers who bring a history of *Accumulated Impact* into your business, agency, or school may have been mistreated based on disability, size, race, sexual orientation, gender, age, religion, accent—you name it.

Train your employees not to fight the customer's perception, but to understand the perception in more depth. The point is not to figure out who is right about what happened. Explain the concept of *Accumulated Impact* so they know that their actions or attitudes,

THE
CLUES

1. COMPANY GUIDELINES   2. LAW   3. YOUR LENS
4. CULTURAL PATTERNS   5. GROUP RADAR
6. COACH   7. ENVIRONMENT

whether intentional or not, could have triggered "history." Then get them to use the same good customer service skills they would use to recover any situation. Many customers are more loyal if you solve a problem for them than if nothing had come up in the first place.

▶ *Give employees skills to deal with cultural history.*

The Customer Is Not Always Right

There are times when mistreatment goes the other way, but it's not often discussed. My clients have described situations where their *customers* have discriminated against, harassed, or offended employees because the *customers* were biased or threatening. Doctors have sexually harassed sales representatives (female and male). Residents in an assisted-living facility have refused to be touched by black employees.

Many businesses are concerned they will lose business if they confront their customers. You must weigh that risk against these potential outcomes:

Losing employees. Employees want their managers to support them. If you don't support them in situations when customers mistreat them based on their identity as a person, you will likely lose their respect.

Losing other customers and employees. Customers and the workforce are increasingly diverse. If they hear that a business doesn't stand up against cultural mistreatment, you run the risk of the word getting around, possibly losing more than one customer.

Losing your credibility. Employees may question your character, affecting other aspects of the business, if you permit customers to discriminate.

These risks are usually much greater to the business than the potential loss of a single customer. Use the following three Clues when the customer is not right in cultural situations:

Clue 1: Look to Your Organization's Cultural Guidelines

Amazingly, there are times when a customer demands someone of a different race, gender, age, and so on. Explain to the customer that this is your employee and he or she is perfectly competent to handle the situation. Your company's belief in the value of diversity is added support. If appropriate, you can explain your organization's core value regarding cultural difference—that

THE **7 CLUES**
1. COMPANY GUIDELINES   2. LAW   3. YOUR LENS
4. CULTURAL PATTERNS   5. GROUP RADAR
6. COACH   7. ENVIRONMENT

employees are given responsibility based on performance, not their cultural makeup.

Clue 2: Turn to the Law

Expect customers to abide by the law, too. The law also supports you, in an exchange with a customer. Legally, you cannot discriminate against your own employee by taking him off an assignment if a customer doesn't like his cultural background.

Clue 6: Coach Performance Cross-Culturally

There may be times when you will want to discuss situations with employees to assure them of your support and to ask for their preference. In the situation of the harassing doctor, the company can lodge a complaint to the doctor or his or her employer. However, you as the manager can ask the employee how she wishes to proceed. In one instance of doctor harassment, some sales reps preferred not to go back to that doctor; others were more confrontive. They told the doctor to stop the offensive behavior, and continued working on the account. You cannot decide this for the employee, lest you discriminate against the employee's ability to make commissions or perform.

▶ *The customer who isn't right is the customer who discriminates.*

The scenarios described above may be more clear-cut than some of the customer-employee situations you will face. Rather than blatant, conscious discrimination, you will likely face circumstances related to the cultural patterns cited in Clue 4, such as *Denial* or being a *Clueless Majority.* At other times, employees may simply not know what to do with cultural difference. Here are some suggestions for the more subtle situations of not knowing, denial, and being a clueless majority.

Subtle Situations

Not knowing.   Recently, two employees in a grocery store told me they didn't know where to find a product in their own store. Not knowing, in this case, is a prescription for losing business, because the store experience becomes too frustrating for the customer to bother going back.

Similarly, when we do our Mystery Patient tours in hospitals presenting cultural challenges to employees, many times they simply do not know how to help or where to direct a customer with a culturally related need. Why do organizations and managers accept this lack of knowledge in regard to cultural needs? The

THE
CLUES

1. COMPANY GUIDELINES   2. LAW   3. YOUR LENS
4. CULTURAL PATTERNS   5. GROUP RADAR
6. COACH   7. ENVIRONMENT

"cultural customer" is just as unlikely to return to organizations that are clueless about culture as I am to go back to stores where clerks don't know their own product.

In fact, in doing our mystery assessments, we find that employees have been trained in service excellence and treating the customer well, but not necessarily in targeting cultural needs. As the health care administrator said, "Nice doesn't cut it" if you are not meeting the customer's need. Try these two Clues in situations where employees don't know how to deal with cross-cultural customers.

Clue 6: Coach Performance Cross-Culturally

When employees simply don't know what to do, training and coaching is appropriate. Depending on the mix of your customers, different procedures and materials will be needed to learn how to meet religious, language, gender-related, and other cultural necessities.

Clue 7: Build a Cross-Cultural Environment

In addition to training, give employees regular information that shows the importance of cultural adaptation to your organization. Consider including culturally related information in your customer satisfaction surveys. Track grievances to see if there is a cultural component to them.

Stoke the positive, too. Build clientele by increasing services to cultural niches. Borders Books is doing this by matching its displays and shelf prominence to authors in the communities it serves. A local outlet in the most affluent, majority black county in the United States features Toni Morrison and Connie Briscoe, prominent black authors, and prime space is devoted to African American fiction and nonfiction. Your information system can track the increases in sales to cultural niches as well as record grievances.

▶ *Train away cultural "I don't knows."*

Denial. One of the more frustrating experiences for culturally diverse people is to complain about differential treatment and to be told that the treatment "had nothing to do with" their race, gender, disability, and so forth. Mostly such conversations end in stalemate because the people arguing are trying to win a debate about who is right. In these situations, use a combination of Clue 5: Use Group-Level Radar and Clue 4: Apply Cross-Cultural Patterns.

You can turn the tendency to deny into an advantage in a customer-related situation. Most people understand the notion of satisfying, even delighting, the customer when she has a problem. Educate your

THE **CLUES** 1. COMPANY GUIDELINES 2. LAW 3. YOUR LENS
4. CULTURAL PATTERNS 5. GROUP RADAR
6. COACH 7. ENVIRONMENT

employees—and yourself—that the natural first response when the customer alleges they have been treated poorly because of their group identity is to deny it. No one wants to be seen as being biased.

Accept that you have biases, and get your employees to accept this fact, too. Then remind them to be calm in situations where they may have made a mistake culturally, and to consider the customer's perception just as they would in a standard service recovery situation.

I have seen hotel workers recover somewhat in such situations. Several times, I have been given special privileges, such as a late hotel checkout, when the colleagues I was traveling with—in each case black women—were denied these privileges. So we went to the front desk together and explained the situation. The desk clerk usually corrected the problem without much fight.

The opportunity is ripe, however, to delight my colleague as a customer by showing cultural skill, rather than simply correcting a mistake. In most situations like this, my colleagues have to fight to get what they want. What I see them getting is a somewhat grudging correction.

Here is another possibility: If your employee were to *acknowledge* the customer's experience that she may have been treated differently, that customer is more likely to be delighted, because most people will deny her claim. The conversation might unfold like this:

Colleague: *When I talked to you, you would not allow me to take a late checkout, but when Mr. Finn talked to you, you gave him the late checkout. What's the difference?*

Desk clerk: *That should never have happened, ma'am. I apologize. I'm also sorry for the inconvenience of your having to come back here and follow up this error. I will put you in for a late check out right now. Is there anything else I can do?*

Colleague: *I'm just frustrated and angry that this happened in the first place. I don't understand why I was treated differently in this case.*

Desk clerk: *It was my mistake, and I can see why you feel you were treated differently. That is not the impression we want to create with our customers. I want you to be delighted with our service and feel respected. I'm actually glad you brought it to my attention.*

You may use different words, but remember these principles:

Don't deny the customer's perception or experience.

THE **CLUES** 7

1. COMPANY GUIDELINES   2. LAW   3. YOUR LENS
4. CULTURAL PATTERNS   5. GROUP RADAR
6. COACH   7. ENVIRONMENT

Aim for delight, not grudging acceptance. Simply correcting the mistake without dialogue is enough to cover you, but doesn't give you the opportunity to surprise, delight, and recover the customer by being willing to hear her frustration with what could be discriminatory treatment. You can shock the person with delight if you actually are willing to hear her talk about being treated differently. Telling her you are glad she brought it up might be the biggest shock of her life.

Don't debate. Demonstrate acceptance. In most cases, it is probably not necessary for you to openly state or admit bias; but you can communicate that you accept her version of events by phrases like "I can see why you feel you were treated differently."

Look to your organization's commitment to customers or to diversity as a beacon (Clue 1). The desk clerk's statement about the impression the hotel wants customers to have is an example of using the organization's principle about service across difference.

▶ *Shock a diverse customer. Thank them for being "too sensitive."*

The Clueless Factor:
Attracting New Customers

Many employees, and organizations, don't know what they don't know about cultural customers. What's worse, they may not know their customers are experiencing problems with them. Here are some actual business problems associated with the situation of being a "clueless majority."

Losing potential customers who could grow your business.   Some customers may not even approach you because they see you as inaccessible culturally (recall the Bank for White People), or some may experience obstacles and decide not to come back.

Spreading bad news about your organization by inadvertently treating customers in a way that drives them off. Recall the Muslim woman who had a bad experience at a hospital which involved, among other things, male orderlies entering her mother's room when she was alone—a major violation to a Muslim woman, but part of a normal routine to the orderly. One bad experience, remember, can become magnified in communities where word-of-mouth is key.

THE CLUES 7	1. COMPANY GUIDELINES 2. LAW 3. YOUR LENS
	4. CULTURAL PATTERNS 5. GROUP RADAR
	6. COACH 7. ENVIRONMENT

Putting the customer in the wrong. This happens any time employees respond in a way that indicates there is no problem or suggests that the culturally different person is being too sensitive.

What can you do to crack the cultural code of customers who you don't know are avoiding you?

Clue 5: Use Group-Level Radar

Start by educating employees that people do get treated differently because of their group membership. You may have trouble convincing some people of this. Those who have experienced discriminatory treatment often understand the group-level concept. But even people who have been treated differently because of, say, their race find it hard to accept that they may have treated someone else differently because of their gender or sexual orientation.

When we speak of clueless situations, we are addressing the tendency not to see because we are *not* members of particular cultural groups. Things we take for granted may be obstacles for others.

"You know what y'all? We're clueless!"

To counter the clueless phenomenon, you can collect examples of the ways diverse people experience your organization. Set up an information system to gather cultural data on customers. Talk with diverse sets of customers regularly. Broaden your definition of culture so that you are considering not just race, but religious groups, age groups, and so on.

Share this information with your employees so they can benefit from hearing examples of how diverse people take in the different aspects of your business. Thinking about customers' cultural difference can encourage employees' ideas for bringing in new customers and satisfying a diverse base with a variety of products and services.

In fact, thinking in niches allows you to attract new customers with very little effort. A group of Muslim women we interviewed were thrilled that they could search a hospital's website for female doctors who spoke their language. This hospital gained a competitive edge simply by providing information on something already there.

You might even counter a seemingly impossible dilemma: bringing in the customers that you don't even know about, like the ones who avoided a Bank for White People. Brainstorm with employees about how to appeal to different cultural niches. You may already

THE 7 CLUES   1. COMPANY GUIDELINES   2. LAW   3. YOUR LENS
4. CULTURAL PATTERNS   5. GROUP RADAR
6. COACH   7. ENVIRONMENT

have an advantage if your workforce itself contains diversity to one degree or another. Again, think beyond race and gender and include other cultural differences.

▶ *Counter cultural cluelessness: think niches.*

The Clueless Factor: Preventing Bad News

One way to get around being clueless to the customer is to focus people on serving the customer. But to prevent bad news about your organization from spreading, focus employees on the fact that the customer is someone who may have a complaint or need that is *culturally* related.

Get employees and your organization to utilize the cultural niche thinking just discussed. But then add a sophisticated twist: proactive use of the cultural patterns in Clue 4.

This doesn't mean you have to segregate customers—some services and treatment are universally appreciated. But cultural niche thinking does mean being alert to how your environment, procedures, or people could cause confusion and frustration for some culturally different customers and be perfectly fine for the mainstream.

Coach your employees to be alert to various cultural niches by using Clue 4's cultural patterns. For example, knowing the Insider/Outsider pattern, a male employee in an auto parts store could be coached to leave his discussion with the boys and immediately greet a lone woman entering the store. In any business, school, or agency setting, if a lone person of another race, age group, or whatever other cultural dimension enters, prevent a potential bad experience by acting with your knowledge of Insider/Outsider dynamics and the other Clues. "Onlys" of any cultural group

THE **7 CLUES**

1. COMPANY GUIDELINES   2. LAW   3. YOUR LENS
4. CULTURAL PATTERNS   5. GROUP RADAR
6. COACH   7. ENVIRONMENT

should get special attention—they are automatically Outsiders.

Employees could also use Clue 4's *Intent versus Outcome* pattern to test many aspects of your business with diverse customers. You could conduct focus groups with cultural groups or parents, asking things like, "Our intent with this form is to get information easily and quickly. How easy and fast is it for you?" You could ask similar *Intent versus Outcome* questions in regard to employee service, your lobby, your programs, and so on.

Use all of Clue 4's patterns in this proactive way. By crossing cultural lines and seeking input, you prevent business problems that can spring from cluelessness.

▶ **Put cultural niche thinking in action. Create good news, and you prevent bad news.**

The Wrap on Scenario 1:
For managing customer-employee cross-cultural problems, use all the Clues; specific Clues are linked to particular customer-employee issues, as shown in this section.

SCENARIO 2

Cultural Cliques

With the growth of diversity, my customers ofen tell me they have "cultural cliques." There are groups who gather to speak their common language; there are racial groups; there are groups formed by being from El Salvador, Rwanda, Russia, or whatever the country of origin.

When addressing the subject of cliques in the workplace, think about how common this cultural gathering process is. Ethnic communities have been doing this "re-gathering" in the United States for years by settling close to one another. From the Italian and Irish immigrants of the 19th and 20th centuries to the growing Russian community in the Twin Cities area, we gather with those with whom we share experience.

Why are cliques at work a problem? Stop and ask yourself that question. It's a good one. In many cases cliques *aren't* a problem. In other cases, if there is a problem, that problem can be handled so much better, depending on the perspective you take.

THE

CLUES

1. COMPANY GUIDELINES   2. LAW   3. YOUR LENS
4. CULTURAL PATTERNS   5. GROUP RADAR
6. COACH   7. ENVIRONMENT

Consider this perspective-changing experience. I remember, somewhat red-faced now, being upset at blacks gathering at the same lunch tables at my college. (Many whites had similar reactions; I have heard this example countless times from others.) I felt excluded. Sometimes I would sit there just to be obstinate.

Years later, I mentioned this to one of my black colleagues. He said, "That's funny. We thought you all were sitting together."

His response startled me. I was so focused on those who were different from the majority (and me) that it had never occurred to me that my group and I could be seen by others as excluding them.

So first clarify your perspective as you think about cliques. Maybe they are not a problem. Even using the word "clique" codes the group as exclusive in a negative way, doesn't it? Sounds like those high school groups who kept you out—and therein lies the first problem.

▶ ***Does your "clique" see your organization as another clique? Who is excluding whom?***

People Like Me: Positive Attraction

In the workplace, a cultural clique would be a problem if there were true exclusion of others; that is, if members of a group were truly refusing to work with, mentor, or share information with people outside their group. In order to ascertain that this is truly the case, you need to get yourself out of the way first.

In the lunchroom, I was convinced that the group of black people was excluding me. Here are a couple of insights: First of all, they weren't thinking about me. They didn't even know me. Second, I found through a couple of later experiences that the greater draw for people who come together, particularly groups who share similar cultural customs *and* treatment by the larger society, is first a positive one, not a negative, exclusionary one.

People who have had to fend for themselves in a foreign country speaking another language know the effort of the experience. It is taxing, mentally and physically, to listen, think, and respond in another language. When you have the chance to return to your native language by meeting someone from your own country, the relief is overwhelming! You can relax.

The same thing is true for people who speak Spanish or Korean or any other language in your workplace. Everything flows so much more easily in your

THE **CLUES** 1. COMPANY GUIDELINES 2. LAW 3. YOUR LENS
4. CULTURAL PATTERNS 5. GROUP RADAR
6. COACH 7. ENVIRONMENT

own language. Beyond that, you are not self-conscious about making mistakes with virtually every sentence you speak.

Extend this ease and comfort out to religious groups, racial groups, gays and lesbians, women, and others. When you are a member of a group that is in the minority by numbers or in an Outsider position by power or influence, you share certain group experiences. There is often great comfort in gathering with like people because they know that the others can understand some key aspects of their experience in the society or workplace. It's likely they won't be questioned as much by members of their own group, told they are too sensitive, or looked at like they are crazy if they mention different treatment based on their group.

Understanding how this shared experience works is the basis for one of the strategies you can use with cultural cliques.

Clue 5: Use Group-Level Radar

I have found that if I regard cultural groupings as a way for people to relax, feel understood, and express themselves without feeling denied, then I don't see these groups excluding me; rather, they are bucking up themselves. The group can serve as an empowering mechanism where expression is free and people are more likely to be themselves. Take a moment to watch a group of women, or a racial group, or language group. See if you notice greater ease, excitement, or energy. That's using your group-level radar.

You want this! Everyone gets some confirmation of himself or herself from a group—whether it is your family, your best friends, a community, your place of worship, your country, or a cultural group. If you think of valuing diversity as a way to grow people by accepting their difference as a positive, then allow cultural groups to flourish. At the very least, people will feel affirmed as individuals. As a bonus, these groups may generate ideas for your business, agency, or school on how to relate to their cultural niche.

You are doing a balancing act here. You want the empowerment of cultural groups without the exclusion. We'll look at the latter next.

▶ *Have cultural affinity work for you. Don't fight it.*

Feeling Left Out?

How do you keep the positive part of cultural group gatherings and lose the exclusive part? Again, this is a

THE **CLUES** 1. COMPANY GUIDELINES 2. LAW 3. YOUR LENS
4. CULTURAL PATTERNS 5. GROUP RADAR
6. COACH 7. ENVIRONMENT

balancing act that families and communities have been dealing with for years. My father's family moved a short distance away from the Irish enclaves of Jersey City. In so doing, there was some loss of connection to an affirming cultural identity. Our move was similar to that of other groups. Black families talk about "not forgetting the community" when you move up socially and economically.

On the other hand, some of those ethnic enclaves have been the most intolerant of others. South Boston's Irish community in the 1970s comes to mind. Many of us often despair of comments in our families about other ethnic and racial groups having this or that negative characteristic or being responsible for the decline of Western civilization.

So when the positive and the potential negative of cultural groups occur in the workplace, don't be surprised. We already have experience with this in the United States. Most of all, don't panic like the potential customer who wanted a consulting intervention because blacks were gathering around the water cooler. Try these suggestions instead:

Clue 3: Clarify Your Cultural Lens
This is a way of "getting yourself out of the way." When you start to worry about the effect of cliques, first make sure that the real problem is not that you or members of your team feel excluded.

Work this out! If the source of the upset is how *you* are viewing the group, you or others may be making up stories about the clique's actions that reflect your view of it. They may have no intention or awareness of excluding you; they may simply be enjoying *being included* in a group of people who share experiences, language, and comfort. If you object to their actions, people might be surprised because they aren't focused on you. Make sure you are not projecting some of your own uneasiness on the group you are observing.

Clue 1: Look to Your Organization's Cultural Guidelines

Then bring to mind your organization's cultural competence principles, as well as its general values. Let's say, for example, that it is essential—for a product to be produced, a patient to be treated, or a child to be educated—that members of your team share information to produce the whole product or service. If you notice that cultural grouping is preventing that sharing of information, then you may have a clique, because members of the group refuse to work with or share information with those outside the clique.

 THE **CLUES** 1. COMPANY GUIDELINES   2. LAW   3. YOUR LENS   4. CULTURAL PATTERNS   5. GROUP RADAR   6. COACH   7. ENVIRONMENT

In other words, don't start intervening, or, for that matter, labeling cultural groups as cliques, until you can clearly see the impacts on how people need to work to accomplish your tasks. First relate the perception of cliques to behaviors that affect work.

Regarding impact on work, then, the classic "old boy network" would be a cultural clique if it excluded women or people of color from promotions, higher positions, and the core decisions that influence a company's product, service, or success. In the long run, exclusions of groups of people would also hurt a company's ability to recruit and retain top talent, eventually damaging its ability to compete.

On the other hand, many organizations hold conferences for women employees to promote an environment that supports their success and advancement. Some men object to those conferences, asking, "Where's the conference for men?"

This case seems to me less about the work being affected and more about men feeling excluded, as I felt in the college cafeteria. Have they wanted a conference before? Do men face promotional or access challenges because they are men? Does the women's conference impede their work? In almost every case, the answer is no.

Analyze the feeling of being left out. Many of us want to be invited to the party, but don't really want to go. See if cultural grouping influences the work negatively (in the case of women's conferences and affinity groups in organizations, there are many positive impacts). Managers, particularly, must be able to make these distinctions.

> ▶ *Are your cliques actually excluding or including? Make sure there is a true business impact.*

The Wrap on Scenario 2:
For managing cultural cliques, use Clue 1: Look to Your Organization's Cultural Guidelines, Clue 3: Clarify Your Cultural Lens, and Clue 5: Use Group-Level Radar.

THE **CLUES**	1. COMPANY GUIDELINES 2. LAW 3. YOUR LENS
	4. CULTURAL PATTERNS 5. GROUP RADAR
	6. COACH 7. ENVIRONMENT

Employee-Employee Relationships

Here are some of the employee-to-employee conflicts/ problems/situations of a cultural nature that I see crop up in working with organizations:

Race card.   Whites feeling people of color are "playing the race card" as an excuse for not receiving a promotion/raise/responsibility. Often people of color who realize many whites feel this way are actually reticent to speak up about differential treatment because they think they won't be believed by whites.

Withholding.   Someone withholding feedback from a manager who is different culturally because he thinks the manager will not "get it" (she won't be open to seeing the influence of her assumptions on her behavior). The employee despairs that it will cost too much in terms of energy, time, or even payback to try to cut through defensiveness.

Fights.   "Fighting" most often involves threats, physical destruction of property, or threatening symbols or emails.

"Do it my way."   People in power positions, culturally or by their organizational role, pull a power play by saying "do it my way." Cultural "do it my ways" are sometimes subtle, but they are felt strongly by those who feel like outsiders culturally. One example is the Christmas holidays for non-Christians. Christians don't have to take vacation for Christmas, whereas many non-Christians do on their holidays. Another cultural "do it my way" includes expectations about conflict. I have heard fears from white people about diversity sessions and an insistence that they be "safe." In my experience, people of color don't fear the conflict as much as they do repercussions for speaking up. The most blatant cultural "do it my way" is the blanket demand by fellow employees that their co-workers speak English at all times.

Insider/Outsider.   Excluding fellow employees not in your cultural group.

Rather than address each of these situations separately, let's look at what is common to these situations so that you can address the roots of cultural conflicts familiar to you. When I think of the conflicts suggested

THE
CLUES
7

1. COMPANY GUIDELINES   2. LAW   3. YOUR LENS
4. CULTURAL PATTERNS   5. GROUP RADAR
6. COACH   7. ENVIRONMENT

by the "race card," ingrained cultural assumptions that discourage dialogue, fights, "do it my ways," and in and out groups, here are the commonalities:

Not seeing the other person's perspective. And, in the case of "do it my way," not *wanting* to see the other person's perspective.

Credibility gulfs, not just gaps. ("He won't get it, so why bother?")

Unwillingness to explore the difference. "Do it my way" or fights are the obvious examples. There are variations on unwillingness to explore, however, that look more like reticence, such as choosing to associate with people just like you or not wanting to expend the energy, time, and risk of exploration.

Therefore, your job as a manager of cultural differences among employees would be to

- make cross-cultural discussion open and desirable as opposed to taboo
- build skills *and* desire to understand a fellow employee's cultural perspective
- ensure credibility/respect, employee to employee, across cultures

We'll start with two segments on promoting openness before moving to skills and credibility.

▶ *Build desire to understand and explore.*

Can We Talk?

Say you are a male leader (women could reverse this process). Can you imagine meeting with the women who work with you and asking for feedback on yourself and the team environment regarding any issues that might be of concern to women?

Start imagining it. Talented women can afford to be choosy about where they want to work. Many are leaving organizations after their firm or agency has invested considerably in them. PricewaterhouseCoopers found, like many other companies, that it had higher turnover among women than men. PepsiCo found turnover among women of color higher than other groups. Pepsi's research showed these women didn't think they had the same relationships with managers as their co-workers did.[13]

A big part of keeping and attracting good, diverse talent is simply allowing people to freely voice their concerns, especially about how they feel about your workplace. After two days of interviews with managers and employees about how diverse people are valued in one of our country's most prestigious institutions, the most repeated complaints were these:

THE **7 CLUES**

1. COMPANY GUIDELINES   2. LAW   3. YOUR LENS
4. CULTURAL PATTERNS   5. GROUP RADAR
6. COACH   7. ENVIRONMENT

"No one wants our opinion" and "Stop fearing our feedback."

Make your workplace a place where cultural issues are just as discussable as differences about how to solve a task. With a task, one person might say, "Here's how I would do it," and another might say, "I would do it

this way," and the two would tackle the differences. With cultural issues, however, the differences in viewpoint are more often hidden.

Insiders culturally (either people in the majority cultural group or those that have greater power by group in the culture) often don't want to discuss cultural assumptions or behaviors because they don't want to be seen as biased. That's natural; it's uncomfortable. Outsider cultural groups are often reluctant to bring up cultural issues for fear of being labeled as making excuses.

So as a leader you've got to break the cultural ice when both sides are reticent.

Clue 7: Build a Cross-Cultural Environment

Put this Clue into practice by asking for cultural feedback. You can establish an environment conducive to cultural discussion by being willing to take feedback from diverse others on your own attitudes and behaviors. Say that you want cultural issues to be a part of your workplace, and state that the last thing you want is for people with concerns and ideas related to cultural differences to hide them.

Then, be ready to get what you ask for!

THE

CLUES

1. COMPANY GUIDELINES   2. LAW   3. YOUR LENS
4. CULTURAL PATTERNS   5. GROUP RADAR
6. COACH   7. ENVIRONMENT

If you invite feedback, you must practice the skills of receiving feedback in order to reinforce the message that it is OK to bring up cultural issues. Your larger goal is to set the atmosphere of openness. So use the "seeking" method, doing whatever you can in the conversation to make sure that you first understand the other's perspective.

Also, take advantage of the time to assess not only concerns, but to ask about things you are doing well, and any ideas that might benefit your organization.

Beyond a meeting of this kind, your ongoing ability to take in culturally related feedback will be important in making cultural issues discussable. Notice what you feel when you do get the feedback. As always, you don't have to agree with the feedback—you are looking for others to make their perspective clear.

A final caution: if you always ignore feedback after hearing it, you may cause the openness gates to close. So heed the message that changing your own behavior and attitudes might be the biggest factor in making cultural issues discussable.

▶ ***To counter "culture talk" reticence, ask for cultural feedback.***

Put Cultural Issues on the Table

Did you know there is culture in lactose? I am not referring to yogurt cultures here. It seems that 80 to 90 percent of adults of African and Asian descent are lactose intolerant.

This fact has come to the attention of the U.S. Department of Agriculture (USDA), which puts out a food pyramid recommending that everyone consume two to three servings of dairy products per day. Now they are aware that cultural differences need to be incorporated into USDA's thinking, research, and products. Millions—an estimated 30 percent of adult Americans—could get regular digestive upset as a result of an assumption by the USDA that all their consumers were the same.

If you are unsure about how to bring diversity to bear in increasing your profit, motivating your class, or developing your agency's effectiveness, begin to open your ears and eyes to the news about culture. Lactose is just one recent example.

The USDA had to think of its consumers in a culturally accurate way. So you might ask your team: Whom are we serving culturally? Do we need to make

THE
CLUES
7

1. COMPANY GUIDELINES   2. LAW   3. YOUR LENS
4. CULTURAL PATTERNS   5. GROUP RADAR
6. COACH   7. ENVIRONMENT

some distinctions? Members of your team may reflect the populations you serve. They may give you some information you haven't thought to ask for.

What about the teams you put on projects? If you say you want a diverse group on a project, that sends a message. You may want, for example, different age groups working together because of the customer profile. How about the presentation team you are sending out? What is the cultural composition of the consumer or client, and should you reflect that in your team?

When you connect diverse cultures to your tasks and model openness, you set an atmosphere where cultural discussion becomes part of the agenda. You legitimize cultural competence. This encourages reticent people to speak up, and puts everyone on notice that dismissing cultural issues is undesirable.

▶ *Take the fear out of bringing up cultural concerns. Make culture part of the agenda.*

Attitudes and Skills for Grownups

"Men are so clueless!"

I've been on the receiving end of that one. And I've laughed at being one of the "accused." But serious cultural pattern watching could help you with serious employee-employee cross-cultural issues.

You're building an environment where cultural issues can be put on the table so that you can prevent these problems. But what you don't want is a table full of kids dumping their glasses of milk. You've got to build some effective cultural skills. Start by using Clue 4.

Clue 4: Apply Cross-Cultural Patterns

The cross-cultural patterns suggest strategies that can work. Skills emerge by being aware of the patterns.

The pattern of *Clueless Majorities*, for example, may seem funny sometimes, but the lack of cultural awareness in the workplace can become a serious barrier if it prompts employees to be unwilling to talk about something their manager does that impedes their work.

Consider two women who are trying to figure out how in the world they will talk to a higher up male whom they feel patronizes them as women. He codes his suggestions as "help," and expects the women to carry out his wishes.

The women want to talk to him about their perception that he is not respecting their equally well-thought-out strategies. Now, of course, his suggestions could be helpful, but the real point is they are not even

THE	1. COMPANY GUIDELINES	2. LAW 3. YOUR LENS
CLUES	4. CULTURAL PATTERNS 5. GROUP RADAR	
	6. COACH 7. ENVIRONMENT	

reaching the point of talking about the bigger issue. From past experiences they think this man is unaware of his own behavior. He will not allow discussion of their *cultural* point: that he has some assumptions about them as women that are influencing his behavior, and he promotes his recommendations as the better thing from a business standpoint.

In other words, the women see him as clueless. More importantly, it's affecting how he treats them, it gets in the way of their work, and they feel he doesn't have the cultural skill to settle the matter without repercussions for them.

So if you have begun to create an environment that puts culture on the table, next make sure your managers and employees have the skills and attitudes to engage in those discussions effectively. In this example, it is crucial that the manager has the skill to hear the women out. Otherwise, they will shut down. Educate your employees about the cross-cultural patterns as a start. Recall the patterns from Clue 4:

- *Clueless Majorities*

- *Insiders and Outsiders*

- *Accumulated Impact*

- *Intent versus Outcome*

- *Denial*

Things like fights, assumptions about playing the race card, and "do it my way" imperatives are symptoms of a real problem—often something on that list of cross-cultural patterns. So focus on these patterns, and, in turn, give your employees the knowledge and skill to work with them. Here follow some quick-hitting ways to crack the cultural code and use the cross-cultural patterns for skill building and problem solving.

▶ *Got a cultural problem? Use pattern*
  awareness.

Problem Prevention: Outsider Progress

You're in an organization like a defense company that has a predominance of certain groups—in this case, 80 percent white, male, and over 40. (Your company's imbalance may not be as great, or maybe it just applies to top managers.) If you're aware of *Clueless Majorities*, especially if you are a member of a majority, translate knowledge of the pattern into action.

Take steps to become aware and make others aware of how people outside those majorities view your

THE

CLUES

1. COMPANY GUIDELINES   2. LAW   3. YOUR LENS
4. CULTURAL PATTERNS   5. GROUP RADAR
6. COACH   7. ENVIRONMENT

performance appraisal system. Track who is getting plum assignments and who is getting promotions. We use focus groups to do this with my clients; you can talk informally to individuals or small groups. Track the history of who has been promoted so that you are aware down the road of the *Accumulated Impact* that may be building for those who aren't rising through the ranks. Do your "diverse others" think your systems are designed for all employees to progress?

▶ **Stop demotivation. Check for cultural blind spots on who's making progress.**

Problem Prevention: "Fight!"

You've got members of your team who fight or don't get along. You need them to work together. You facilitate some discussions with them, and you begin to "de-focus" their tendency to emphasize their latest transgressions with each other. You point out, or help them to see, the *Accumulated Impact* that is influencing them every time they get in a discussion. Their history biases their openness to hearing each other. You steer them to focus on the history first, rather than the current issue. Here is an example:

John:
(black man)
I'm tired of being told I'm "arrogant," everytime I make a suggestion around here.

Tom:
(white man)

> *If each "suggestion" weren't paired with telling me "I don't get it" every time, maybe you'd get somewhere.*

You:

> *Time out. We're going around the barn again. I want you guys to see the pattern that is locking these arguments in place. John, you mentioned the word arrogant. Is there something about that word that gets you— maybe something beyond Tom here?*

John:

> *Yes, I've heard it for years to describe me and other black men, even if we are respectful in our comments.*

You:

> *Thank you. And Tom, you mentioned "not getting it." How do you take that in, maybe beyond just John's saying it?*

Tom:

> *I feel like he's lumping me in with all white men and accusing me of being biased.*

You:

> *OK. Can you both see how your words are being received? Each of you is tapping into the other's history or associations with larger issues, like bias. It's no wonder you can't focus on the actual suggestion or work issue.*

THE

CLUES

7

1. COMPANY GUIDELINES   2. LAW   3. YOUR LENS
4. CULTURAL PATTERNS   5. GROUP RADAR
6. COACH   7. ENVIRONMENT

> *Let's talk a bit about the larger impact you*
> *are both triggering and see how we can stop*
> *the cycle.*

▶ *Fighters don't ignore the past. Neither*
should problem solvers.

Problem Prevention:
"You Treat Us Differently"

You have people who, as a group, feel they have been treated differently because of their race. What you or the organization have done consistently is to point out how the treatment is not racial, it is something else.

Since this *Denial* is not working (even if you still believe you are right, you can see you have a stalemate), and in fact may be contributing to the *Accumulated Impact* for the ones complaining, you decide to use the *Intent versus Outcome* tool. You now have a different discussion. When they discuss what has happened in the past, you want to know what the *outcome* was for them. You clarify, asking things like, "So the way you experienced the policy change was . . ." or "So what was the outcome for you, as you see it?"

Separating intent from outcome allows you to move things forward from the stalemate because you are beginning to untie the knot. You feel your *intent* was positive; however, if you keep stressing that, someone who didn't take it that way won't feel the way he or she experienced your action is ever heard.

Stay comfortable inside about your intent, but leave it inside for the moment. Understanding that people can take things differently than we intend—and magnifying that when different cultures are involved—changes your mindset. Become an explorer of what the outcome was for *them*. Then your sincerity is felt on the other side.

Before using *Intent versus Outcome* at work, practice it at home with a partner or child. Home life has provided opportunity for its application since time immemorial! Then begin teaching your employees to make the distinction.

Timing is everything with this tool. The mistake most people make is they state their intent too soon. "No, no, that's not what I meant by 'girls'; I was trying to compliment you." Don't talk about your intent until you feel the outcome for the other person has been fully acknowledged.

▶ *Got a cultural problem? Store intention, explore outcomes.*

THE **CLUES**

1. COMPANY GUIDELINES   2. LAW   3. YOUR LENS
4. CULTURAL PATTERNS   5. GROUP RADAR
6. COACH   7. ENVIRONMENT

Coaching Cultural R-E-S-P-E-C-T

Rodney Dangerfield couldn't "get no respect." Aretha Franklin wanted it. Cultural groups want it, too. Hidden beneath the assumptions, the race cards, and the notions that majority groups won't "get it" is a loss of R-E-S-P-E-C-T, triggered by cultural differences. The example of the women feeling patronized by their male manager who offers "help" is subtle cultural conflict, but its base is not feeling respected.

We've just covered the basic building blocks (openness and skills) for solving employee-to-employee cross-cultural problems. There is one other vital need: an accompanying attitude of core respect and credibility across cultures.

Most respect has to be earned; but cultural difference often adds an extra hurdle for groups that are stereotyped, mistrusted, or unknown by others. When there are employee-to-employee cultural problems, or simply a lack of mixing across cultures, you may need to coach respect (Clue 6).

Coaching cultural respect puts a leader front and center in our society in a unique way. At work, people of different cultures work together. That's not always so in the greater society, where living apart from other cultures is common, where heterosexuals can choose not to associate with gay people, where religions and clubs congregate with their own.

Leaders are expected to bring these people—who choose not to cross lines in their personal lives—together and achieve a goal in the workplace. Think about that. High expectations!

Bringing cultures together is another one of those roles for which we don't train most leaders. So what are some ways that you can promote fundamental respect across cultures, particularly if some of the cross-cultural doubts like stereotypes and mistrust are present? Consider rotation, paying attention to patterns, positioning for success, and handling ingrained disrespect.

Rotate. Pay attention to the assumptions you hear bandied about, and use rotations and projects to put people together. If small groups are excluding others, use workplace assignments to mix people and give employees a fresh experience of others. If you hear majority group members stereotyping cultural groups or making assumptions, check whether they are getting enough exposure to one another and create opportunities where they will have to mix.

For some people, exposure to difference brings them around. They are forced to learn about the world of the "other." That may be all it takes. For others, that is not the case. That's where your coaching comes in.

▶ *Don't let uninformed disrespect stand—mix.*

Pay attention. Be alert to the interactions of the cross-cultural teams you have.

Start by catching people practicing cultural competence well. Reinforce their actions positively.

> *Ted's curriculum this year includes segments on culturally diverse approaches to the study of science. Let's talk about how other staff might put diversity in their lesson plans.*

> *Sandra, thank you for pointing out how our discussion style here may be preventing our ESL [English-as-a-second-language] employees from giving ideas for new products. That could significantly influence our business.*

Or, if you notice someone in knee-jerk denial about a bias that may be clouding their judgment, ask them to slow down and take another look. Pay particular attention to Insider group dynamics. Insider group members are often unaware of what Outsider groups see and experience.

Employee: *We don't have any problems with people with disabilities.*

You: *That may be true. But since we have no identified people with disabilities on our team, and very few in the company, how can we be sure we have no problems? For all I know, none apply as employees because they don't know us*

> *or they see no one with a disability here. We*
> *may be losing customers with disabilities for*
> *the same reason.*

Let's assume that you have educated your group about denial and the other cross-cultural patterns. You can facilitate actively or from the sidelines. With *Intent versus Outcome,* you could help the group to parse out what each side's intent was, as well as outcome.

You could have women speak to *Accumulated Impact,* talking about how a male co-worker's attempts

- Group vs. Individual
- Accumulated Impact
- Intent vs. Outcome

"Let's look at this another way."

to "help" relate to their experiences as women. You could ask this man to think about Clue 5: Use Group-Level Radar by saying:

> *OK, you thought you were helping each person at the* individual *level. What are they telling you about your impact at the* group *level—the impact on them as women? Which level seems to be carrying more weight for them?*

Pay attention, and be prepared to use the Clues and patterns in these ways to help people work through problems. Then get them to use the Clues as tools to handle cross-cultural situations.

▶ *Coaching respect requires activating your cultural radar.*

Set them up to succeed. Picture the all-important presentation to top management. I was due to make this presentation, based on in-depth research that I conducted with a team of people. I was the one with the most knowledge of the information, so the customer wanted me to make the presentation.

The customer, however, switched the date of the presentation twice. Finally on the third date they requested I was not available. I asked a female colleague to substitute for me. We prepared her. Then the date got switched again to a time that I *was* available.

Given that we were now both prepared, I thought we should present together. (Big mistake!) As the presentation drew near, the customer asked that I present the data, saying that because I had been so intimately involved, it made sense. I kept my colleague as part of the presentation, but her role was diminished to facilitating discussion.

Some time later, the customer asked that we not use my colleague again on the project. Though other reasons were given, I believe I contributed to this outcome by limiting her role on presentation day. This meant that she did not appear as influential and competent as I knew her to be.

When you set up diverse teams and ask people to take on new roles, make sure you give them the tools and authority they will need. Don't subordinate people who may have already been subordinated in society by putting them in roles that limit their ability to shine.

▶ *Think about how you position your Outsiders.*

THE **7 CLUES**

1. COMPANY GUIDELINES   2. LAW   3. YOUR LENS
4. CULTURAL PATTERNS   5. GROUP RADAR
6. COACH   7. ENVIRONMENT

Handling ingrained disrespect.   Remember the Middle Eastern men who wouldn't respect the authority of their female, Iranian supervisor? What is the best way to manage a problem netted in a web of ingrained gender role beliefs?

The basic answer is to work the behaviors, not the beliefs. When you are in doubt on any cultural dilemma, distinguishing behaviors and beliefs can help. Most companies are not trying to change employee beliefs. They can, however, expect behavior consistent with their core principles regarding cultural difference. So look to your organization's cultural guidelines (Clue 1).

The boundary of the workplace—with its expectations for performance—gives you greater ability to influence team members whose biases may be creeping into their behaviors. Don't just talk to the men about "respecting" their female supervisor. Break down respect into measurable behaviors. If men are withholding information, talk about your expectations for sharing information. If disrespect shows up in how they talk to her in front of others, be clear on what the impact of that talk is. Does it undermine her authority with the customer or other employees? Does it force her to spend time and energy on their behavior, time that could be better spent focusing on the organization's goals?

Most organizations have principles for cultural competence along the lines of "valuing and utilizing cultural differences in the service of our customers and employees." Clarify how disrespect hurts your organization's mission and how it is contrary to valuing difference. Then specify the behaviors desired.

▶ *For culturally ingrained disrespect, clarify respect. Link it to a task.*

The Wrap on Scenario 3:

To solve employee-employee cross-cultural problems, use Clue 7: Build a Cross-Cultural Environment, Clue 4: Apply Cross-Cultural Patterns, Clue 6: Coach Performance Cross-Culturally, and Clue 1: Look to Your Organization's Cultural Guidelines.

THE **CLUES** 1. COMPANY GUIDELINES 2. LAW 3. YOUR LENS
4. CULTURAL PATTERNS 5. GROUP RADAR
6. COACH 7. ENVIRONMENT

Favoritism and Glass Ceilings

Count.

Count, and you will be halfway toward managing cultural favoritism. Counting is what a surprising number of your employees do as they look up in your organization. Your diverse employees count who is at the top of your organization, and they round out their census from myriad perspectives: how old the top ones are, what religion they are, their race and gender, who they know, you name it.

Just as our definition of cultural groups has been broad, so the ways employees see favoritism is legion. The classic cultural cases are racial and gender-specific, where women and outsider groups see little hope for advancement beyond a certain organizational level. As they look up, they see only white men among the top managers. One major corporation is a good example. Its top 400 managers are predominantly white and male. What's more, in a recent round of promotions for 12 top positions, all 12 were given to white men. And this is a company quite committed to a diversity effort.

Talk to employees, however, and you will see perceptions of favoritism and ceilings from all angles, not just race and gender. A gay man hoping to become a partner at a prestigious firm elects not to take his significant other to a company party, knowing there are no openly gay partners at the firm. A foundation board of directors knows that it is serving low-income populations, but discusses openly that all of its members are very well off financially, thus likely to miss the needs of its customers. A comment from a survey at a defense contractor notes that the only people one sees at the top are generals, so employees doubtlessly ask themselves, "How far can I go?"

For many people, changing the perception of favoritism toward the "in" crowd is an organizational culture issue: to change the perception, you need to change the culture.

This is a book for individual leaders, so I will leave the bulk of organizational culture change to the many books on that subject. Yet favoritism toward cultural and other groups does affect your culturally diverse employees—their motivation, their hopes, their desire to stay with your company, their belief in whether the company can change, and their energy. So we can't leave favoritism and glass ceilings out of what you can do every day as a leader of diverse people. You are cracking a code of silence and resignation when you address perceptions of favoritism. It is a big issue in

THE
CLUES   1. COMPANY GUIDELINES   2. LAW   3. YOUR LENS
     4. CULTURAL PATTERNS   5. GROUP RADAR
       6. COACH   7. ENVIRONMENT

organizations. Here are some ideas for leading people who see favoritism as a block.

▶ *What do your diverse employees see when they look up? Do you know?*

Remember Softball

Many of us remember being the outsider simply by recalling getting picked last for the pickup softball game. I know this because so many of my customers cite this example!

Create a solid personal base for managing favoritism by remembering your own outsider experiences. Start by identifying, if you can, with the gut-level experience that one's advancement might be limited by cultural group identity. Recall any time that your identity as a member of a group, not as an individual, may have blocked good assignments or possibilities.

Many people in Outsider cultural groups can recall such experiences easily. If you belong to predominantly Insider groups in society you may still have had episodes where you felt you were stymied because you were different. A young white female consultant, though part of the Insider racial group in the United States, cited a regular bias against her age. An older customer said to her, "What can you tell me, being so young?"

Remembering your own experiences helps keep you as a leader from being dismissive of perceptions of glass ceilings. If you know what favoritism is like, even in a one-time episode, your response can be more connected to your culturally diverse employees.

▶ *You were an Outsider once.*

Apply Windex

If you can't recall a time when you faced the glass ceiling, remember *Clueless Majorities* (see Clue 4: Apply Cross-Cultural Patterns). If you think someone who makes a cultural claim about glass ceilings is off the mark, check first whether not belonging to their group may naturally put you in the clueless category. Here are some steps to clean the glass and raise your cultural awareness.

Don't deny the perception. Assume that you are clueless about other cultures' perceptions. Knowing that being unaware is common when you are outside a particular group, you may be more likely to listen to

THE
CLUES
1. COMPANY GUIDELINES   2. LAW   3. YOUR LENS
4. CULTURAL PATTERNS   5. GROUP RADAR
6. COACH   7. ENVIRONMENT

the other person's perception. Start by not denying what they say.

Ask "What are you seeing?" Try to see what your employees are seeing as best you can. Ask for examples. At AOL,[14] employees believed their case for favoritism and glass ceilings was reinforced by these observations:

- None of the senior executives were people of color.

- Hiring and promotion showed a pattern of bringing on and advancing white people.

- People of color felt they were included in meetings with external customers (to show diversity), but kept out of key internal meetings where decisions were made.

- One of the primary social events sanctioned by the company was the Friday beer bashes, where women felt they were expected to go along with male bar behavior.

Be careful and skillful, however, when you ask for examples. There is a tendency to dismiss them, one-by-one, if you disagree. Don't create this kind of academic grilling atmosphere. You are seeking examples in order to understand.

Begin *Tracking.*™ Notice what others are seeing by tracking by cultural group. Begin looking for yourself —at meetings, in policies, in company practices—to see if there is a different impact for diverse groups. Using the AOL scenario, you could track:

- Who heads up important projects?

- Which racial and gender groups are more predominant in support roles and groups?

- Which groups predominate among those who are hired and promoted?

- Do our top people match our customers?

▶ *Turn "clueless" into strategies: accept, ask, track.*

Do Salad Makers Have Potential?

Cultural difference heightens the risk of favoritism for some and lack of opportunity for others. It's natural— we tend to gravitate toward those who are like us, and difference often causes discomfort or barriers. The

	1. COMPANY GUIDELINES	2. LAW	3. YOUR LENS
THE **CLUES**	4. CULTURAL PATTERNS	5. GROUP RADAR
	6. COACH	7. ENVIRONMENT

salad makers cited earlier (see "Understand Internalized Oppression" under Clue 6: Coach Performance Cross-Culturally), all Latino, had virtually no contact with the general manager of the restaurant. Language difference was first and foremost in creating the barrier, but there were also differences in social class, national origin, and hierarchical level—a major, subtle separator in most organizations.

The salad makers were also totally removed physically from the main action in the company—where the customers ate. Their position, location, language, class, and national origin limited both their knowledge of the company and their ability to progress.

The leader of a multicultural workforce has, therefore, a crucial role in making sure these natural cultural and organizational invisible ceilings are not holding people back. Your role as a developer becomes more vital when your workforce is diverse.

Despite the crush of daily events, think more long term, and envision the kind of workplace you want. Imagine your area as one that grows people. If your workplace is to be one where everyone is growing and learning, then you must first ask, "How can each person grow and progress?" This requires that you and your managers know your employees well—their talents, backgrounds, and desires—so that all can contribute their fullest and see possibilities for themselves.

That may sound like commonsense leadership, but when you can't speak your employee's language, or when race or physical ability or sexual orientation separate you from your employees, opening up growth opportunities becomes a paramount concern.

Make opportunity real and tangible for everyone, so each person can see clearly what is possible to achieve in your workplace. Find out people's strengths and goals, make plans with them, then follow up. People will see opportunity in their organization if you, the individual leader, are working to make your area a place where growth is possible for everyone.

▶ *Make your workplace a "potential place."*

Use Your Influence . . . and Your Influencers

Don't give up on your ability to influence the larger culture. The steps you take toward understanding how your diverse employees see the company, and whether favoritism thrives there, can give you insights to communicate to your colleagues and senior management.

One idea is simply to find out what the company is doing regarding opportunity for diverse employees.

THE 7 CLUES	1. COMPANY GUIDELINES 2. LAW 3. YOUR LENS
	4. CULTURAL PATTERNS 5. GROUP RADAR
	6. COACH 7. ENVIRONMENT

You can make a business case by comparing the cultural makeup of your customers or constituents to the cultural makeup of your employee population, with particular attention to the decision-making levels.

Do you see any important discrepancies between your customers and the organization? If so, make an argument for making more opportunity available for people who are underrepresented.

The other question to ask is, "How does a lack of diversity at upper levels affect employee openness?" How honest do you and your colleagues believe employees can be about their concerns? Are they like the gay man who felt he couldn't bring his partner to a party at his firm without jeopardizing his ability to advance? The ability to be open is a crucial determinant of success with cultural diversity.

Recruitment is another area where the question "What are we doing?" is a useful one. If your employee and management ranks are homogeneous to the extent that diverse customers may choose to go elsewhere, what does the pipeline coming in look like? Too often I hear the response that "we just can't find any qualified minorities."

This is an area where cluelessness may reign and be reinforced by the clueless. We often find that when one begins to dig into the recruitment area, the answers to the questions, "Where are you looking?" and "Who is doing the looking?" drive the organization's lack of results.

Organizations tend to recruit in the places they have recruited before, thus getting the same people, by group, that they got before. Diverse recruiters can help. They will question the assumption that there are "no qualified X" because they already know qualified Xs or know how to find them.

In sum, tackling favoritism and glass ceiling issues comes down to responding to these questions: Are we matching our customers' diversity? Are we allowing our diverse employees to influence our direction? Or are our homogeneity and myopia at the top affecting our ability to become more capable culturally?

▶ *Call in the cultural reinforcements: your diverse customers and employees.*

The Wrap on Scenario 4:
The suggestions in this segment on perception of glass ceilings and favoritism correspond to Clue 3: Clarify Your Cultural Lens, Clue 5: Use Your Group-Level Radar, and Clue 7: Build a Cross-Cultural Environment.

THE CLUES	1. COMPANY GUIDELINES 2. LAW 3. YOUR LENS
	4. CULTURAL PATTERNS 5. GROUP RADAR
	6. COACH 7. ENVIRONMENT

"You're in America. Speak English"

I am amazed at how hot an issue language is among my customers. Most people assume that race and sexual orientation win the gold for controversy and heat, and often they do, but speaking other languages makes many people in the United States indignant, as if it is unjust to speak another language in the workplace. Others make assumptions about the language speakers that make them out to be gossipers or lazy.

These are common statements made about people speaking another language in the workplace:

We're in America. Speak English!

They don't even make an effort to learn English.

I know they're talking about me when they speak their own language.

The law will help you in addressing language issues. But as you can see, you are managing not only a problem to be solved, but also high emotion. People who make these statements appear threatened by those who speak another language. It is as if language is the place where they have decided to dig the foxholes in the battle for the culture. Meanwhile our European counterparts cross national lines readily, speaking two or three languages with ease while getting to the business at hand.

Your challenge is that you want to value and keep both the people who object and the people who are multilingual, assuming performance is good on both sides. Yet another challenge might be that you agree with the foxhole diggers. That's OK, but it doesn't absolve you from addressing this increasing debate. As a leader, you still have to deal with the divide language seems to provoke, so here are some tips that are helpful regardless of your personal feelings.

▶ *Language is hot. Make sure you're not.*

Don't Return Gifts

Let's assume your organization has some commitment to diversity and has developed a policy similar to this one: "the organization will embrace customer and employee cultural differences." If so, then you don't want to shut down people speaking another language because some others don't like hearing another language "in America."

THE
CLUES

1. COMPANY GUIDELINES   2. LAW   3. YOUR LENS
4. CULTURAL PATTERNS   5. GROUP RADAR
6. COACH   7. ENVIRONMENT

One of the clearest reasons why you don't want to clamp down on other languages is business related. Suppose you have customers who speak another language, and they need help. How can you tell an employee to stop speaking their language, and then later ask them to help the business by speaking it? You will confuse them, have them walking on eggshells, and make them resentful.

You have a gift in a multilingual employee when you are serving an increasingly global marketplace and an increasingly diverse citizenry. As you consider policies and responses regarding language in the workplace, start with an attitude that says, "I want this skill in my area."

▶ *Value your employees' cultural gifts—particularly when you get them for free.*

Be Lawful

If there is a good reason why you must limit the use of other languages—and I urge you to make sure it is a business reason, not a matter of cultural preference—then the law helps you split the difference between the multilingual employees and the objectors. (Use Clue 2.)

As a manager you cannot make a blanket statement that other languages cannot be spoken in the workplace. That could violate the law; however, you can say that there are times when English will be spoken, such as in dealing with English-speaking customers. You must clarify the specific business reasons, the business situations, and any consequences for not using English.

Because many people have a strong preference in the United States that English be spoken, be clear that business considerations must drive your limitation on any use of another language. That may require revisiting Clue 3: Clarify Your Cultural Lens. It is a *cultural preference*, not the law, that English be spoken at all times, and as a manager you and the organization can be sued for insisting on it as a blanket requirement.

▶ **With language, the law is your friend.**
Use it to balance emotion.

Why Limit Growth?

The business world is more multicultural now. U.S. companies compete globally; government agencies and schools serve a remarkable array of cultures; we meet or see through the Internet and media people from

THE **7 CLUES**
1. COMPANY GUIDELINES   2. LAW   3. YOUR LENS
4. CULTURAL PATTERNS   5. GROUP RADAR
6. COACH   7. ENVIRONMENT

many other countries; our grocery shelves are stacked with foods from all over the world.

Prepare and grow employees for this multicultural world. Besides analyzing, selling, counting, creating, teaching, or computing, employees also need skills to deal with difference. If a person objects to hearing another language, in today's world you may want to challenge their lack of openness, rather than limit the language speakers. That's where coaching will come in (see "Coaching in Tongues" below).

Meanwhile, you want to build an environment that values difference (Clue 7). If you truly see that language is being used as a way to divide people, then use some team building techniques for bringing people together. One of those techniques is to have a clear set of values and a vision or image of the team working together. Top on that list should be the idea of embracing difference. Limiting languages spoken is the opposite of that.

So is using language to exclude or gossip. The first thing you can do to address language divides is to be nonreactive and calm. Second, you can insist that exclusion and gossip are not part of your vision. Make that part of the vision real by facilitating dialogues across the language groups or by putting members of each group on common projects.

▶ *Put valuing of difference into action.*
Cross language divides.

Coaching in Tongues

Coaching often involves getting people to become a bigger version of themselves. As a manager of diverse cultures, you may have to coach people past some of their assumptions about cultural issues that may be keeping them from performing their best (Clue 6). That may take some confronting. On language (and other) issues, do the following:

Be alert to assumptions.   Statements about other cultures are often made with great certitude. Because we often lack contact with or knowledge of other cultures, many of these statements have no basis in fact. You can count on inaccuracies with cultural difference. Don't let bravado fool you.

Consider the assumption "they're talking about me" when others speak in their own language. How does the person know that—particularly since he can't understand the language? What about "They don't make an effort to learn English"? Does this person tail their co-worker 24 hours a day?

When you hear assumptions like this, put your first questions to the one making them. Feelings of being

THE
CLUES

1. COMPANY GUIDELINES   2. LAW   3. YOUR LENS
4. CULTURAL PATTERNS   5. GROUP RADAR
6. COACH   7. ENVIRONMENT

excluded or threatened, without knowledge of what is going on, often provoke people to make up stories. Help them understand that they are making an assumption. Ask them what behavior provoked the assumption, and work with them to identify the difference between the two.

Ask "So what?" This question is not often asked regarding language. If someone is speaking another language in the workplace, so what? Is the work compromised, the team hurt, the customer not served? Here again, you should wade through the assumptions. One of the assumptions might simply be that it is bad to speak another language in the workplace. Question that assumption. Why is that a negative?

If you are going to limit languages spoken, make sure you can clearly see a behavior that is hurting the business in some way.

You may say that the team is hurt if one member objects to the other language. Consider that the team may be hurt more if foreign language speakers now have to hide a part of themselves. The team would not be hurt unless the one objecting is letting it hurt him or herself. If that person makes the assumption that "they're talking about me," try the following:

- Speak to that individual about the pitfalls of assuming (need I repeat, "when you assume, you make an *ass* out of *u* and *me*"?).

- Ask them the "so what" question. Even if they are talking about you, what's the problem?

- Offer to facilitate a discussion with multilingual people in order to explore the assumption.

Objections to other languages being spoken are loaded with political and personal beliefs. You may share some of those beliefs, which can make your job as a multicultural manager harder. Separate out the business issues by using the Clues suggested. Check your own and others' assumptions first. If a dialogue across language lines is needed, have it, but facilitate the dialogue skillfully or bring in someone who can.

Above all, keep a vision for embracing difference in mind. Your employees may just be a part of the transition to a more accepting, diverse society that is influencing the United States and the whole world.

▶ *Cut through language assumptions.*
English isn't going away.

THE
CLUES

1. COMPANY GUIDELINES   2. LAW   3. YOUR LENS
4. CULTURAL PATTERNS   5. GROUP RADAR
6. COACH   7. ENVIRONMENT

Leading People Who Speak Another Language

Many organizations, hotels and restaurants are prime examples, have employees who speak a language different from their manager. In office environments, I more often encounter professionals who have trouble understanding people who speak English with a foreign accent (to be discussed in the next segment).

What if you can't speak your employee's native tongue, and he can't speak yours? Certainly there are practical solutions to the immediate language problem (interpreters, co-workers who can translate), but here's the real issue for you as a manager of non-English speakers: does the language barrier stunt these employees' ability to grow and block opportunity for them?

The Value of Small Talk

Think practically, not personally. You may be doing nothing intentionally to impede these employees, but their inability to speak with you maroons non-English speakers on a limiting workplace island. We take for granted the ability to converse, to make small talk. Small talk gives us a more complete picture of the person with whom we are speaking—what their mannerisms mean, what their tone indicates, the kind of humor they use.

When I spoke to Latino workers in a restaurant some time back, they felt the head chef was insensitive. They cited as an example his bursting into their area and simply saying, "I need 40 salads!"

I thought the chef was a nice man, concerned about his employees. The salad makers didn't. Their interactions with the chef were limited, so his demands formed their impression, which wasn't softened by conversation with the chef. They couldn't talk to each other.

The same is true in any manager-employee relationship. If we don't speak the same language, we interact less. We get the same result with race and organizational barriers. These barriers unintentionally limited the African American woman who was an active leader at church but a quiet support person at work; managers were unaware of her talents. The same goes for us when we can't speak to our employees.

The problem of not speaking the language is therefore not simply linguistic. It has deeper implications for employee growth and effectiveness, and ultimately business results.

▶ *Are language barriers limiting your impression of employee potential?*

THE **CLUES**   1. COMPANY GUIDELINES   2. LAW   3. YOUR LENS
4. CULTURAL PATTERNS   5. GROUP RADAR
6. COACH   7. ENVIRONMENT

The Opportunity Language

What can you do if you lead people who don't speak your language?

Use Clue 4: Apply Cross-Cultural Patterns. Recall the pattern of *Insiders and Outsiders.* People who don't speak English or who are not native to the country are definitely an outsider group in the workplace. They can't speak and be understood by many people, their ideas are usually not heard, and their jobs and opportunities are limited. They are likely to be reluctant to speak out.

All these dynamics limit the potential of your non-English speakers. Here are some things you can try to counter the isolating forces that could keep this group unempowered:

Find ways to have the core development conversations that you would have with any employee. Maybe you will need an interpreter. However you do it, you want to know their goals, their background, and their other talents.

You may have to be patient. They may not trust you at first. It's possible they have never had a manager ask them what *they* want from their job. Stick with it by showing, over time, that you mean it. Follow up the conversation with actions and more discussion.

Look for growth opportunities, rotations, and other challenges. Are salad makers destined to be salad makers forever because they can't speak English . . . right now? If you are committed to making your area a place where everyone grows, then look for ways that your "salad makers" can grow, step-by-step.

Try to learn at least a few expressions in the language of your non-English speakers. This symbolically evens the Insider/Outsider score a little by showing that you are willing to be a bit vulnerable, which is the everyday position of the foreign language speakers.

Talk with employees about whether they would like to learn English.   Are there ways you can help with this? Think about "skilling up" your current employees with English and other skills as a way to reduce recruiting costs for new Outsiders.

▶ *Can't speak their language? Speak opportunity and dreams instead.*

THE
CLUES

1. COMPANY GUIDELINES   2. LAW   3. YOUR LENS
4. CULTURAL PATTERNS   5. GROUP RADAR
6. COACH   7. ENVIRONMENT

"I Don't Have an Accent. You Do"

My friend Rita from Rhode Island gets asked all the time, "Where'd you get that accent?" Often she says, "I don't have an accent. You do."

What constitutes "different" is often in the eye of the beholder. When that difference becomes the subject of whether someone is valued or needs to change, then you as a manager have things beyond accents to manage. Your job includes seeing the cultural landscape more clearly, knowing whether your employee with a foreign accent is experiencing *Accumulated Impact,* and deciding on actions that go beyond the obvious.

Whose Problem Is It Anyway?

People deal with the problem of heavily accented English throughout my customer base in the United States. The most common scenario is the professional meeting or conference call. I am amazed at how frustrated the native English-speaking listeners become. Not understanding, and waiting for people to express themselves, feels excruciating to some.

The listeners are not the only ones frustrated.

An African security guard at a U.S. hospital says he is surprised at the trouble Americans have understanding accented English. "I don't mind if they don't understand me and ask me to repeat," says he, "but I notice that when I also have to understand English from someone who is foreign to *me*, I have much less difficulty than the Americans."

It is possible that our history of generally not learning other languages and expecting others to speak English has made us somewhat lazy in doing the work of understanding accents. But the standard response in organizations has been to provide tutoring for the speaker to "correct" the accent. Some ESL speakers welcome the help, and in the end, tutoring may be part of the solution.

Be more skillful and complete, however, in dealing with the issue of accents. The work of understanding accents includes not only being patient, but also "tuning in" more. Tuning in means listening better to each word, but it also means listening for context; that is, if you can't pick up every word, can you get the meaning from the surrounding words?

▶ *Accents are spoken and heard. Coach the speakers and the listeners.*

THE 7 CLUES	1. COMPANY GUIDELINES 2. LAW 3. YOUR LENS
	4. CULTURAL PATTERNS 5. GROUP RADAR
	6. COACH 7. ENVIRONMENT

"What She Means to Say Is . . ."

Stories from ESL speakers about reactions to their accents are at times surprisingly hurtful and demeaning. Several, including highly degreed, educated people, have felt they have been labeled as stupid by native English speakers, simply because of their accents. A woman at a pharmaceutical company spoke about co-workers constantly speaking for her after she spoke, saying, "What she means to say is . . ." The *Accumulated Impact* of people speaking for her was strong. She cried while relating the story.

Assuming that you know a person's intent—and speaking for them—is classic Insider behavior. Be alert for this "caretaking" of your ESL speakers; it's often not perceived as helpful, but hurtful. Instead of speaking for someone, use openness and humility. "I'm sorry, Jean, I didn't understand this part of what you said."

This stance of acknowledging that *you* didn't get it once again evens the vulnerability with the Outsider. The skill, therefore, is to remember that being an ESL speaker is inherently subordinating. It is easy to feel "one down" or "less than." Don't speak for her. Don't bypass her input because it is hard to understand. Alert your employees if you see they are speaking for someone or are not trying hard enough to listen.

You may still want to discuss with ESL speakers the idea of help with their accent if you and they agree that it is a block to their progress. Just don't make this your

only strategy. Combine it with other actions that take
Insider and Outsider dynamics into account.

▶ *People with accents like speaking for
themselves.*

The Wrap on Scenario 5:
*The suggestions in this segment on "You're in America. Speak English"
correspond to Clue 1: Look to Your Organization's Cultural Guidelines,
Clue 2: Turn to the Law, Clue 4: Apply Cross-Cultural Patterns, Clue 6:
Coach Performance Cross-Culturally, and Clue 7: Build a Cross-Cultural
Environment.*

THE CLUES	1. COMPANY GUIDELINES 2. LAW 3. YOUR LENS
	4. CULTURAL PATTERNS 5. GROUP RADAR
	6. COACH 7. ENVIRONMENT

Political Correctness

Every one of my customers has a group—sometimes large—who sees cultural competence work as fluff, not related to the work of the organization. Managers who are concerned about cultural issues worry that these groups will sabotage their organizations' efforts, so the topic of political correctness (PC) becomes important to address.

There are simple, logical arguments you can make to counter the notion that cultural competence work is unnecessary or a burden. I'll list those later. But if logic did the trick, the issue of political correctness wouldn't be an issue at all.

Crawling up the Courthouse Steps

Logical arguments for cultural competence don't always work—at least at the beginning—because decrying "This is all PC!" has more to do with emotion than logic. The emotional objections seem to be:

Feeling restricted.   People may complain, "You can't joke around here anymore," or "I have to walk on eggshells."

Having to change. Many people feel put off by being asked to change behavior. And for many of us, it's just plain hard!

Having to see another point of view. It takes emotional skills such as openness and sympathy to be able to do this. Not everyone has been trained to do this effectively.

Most of my customers are very concerned about employees who resist a cultural competence effort, so they try using logical arguments to convince them (for example, presenting the business case for diversity). It often doesn't work. I find it is better to postpone the logic and meet the emotional resistance first. Try using Clues #3 and #4.

Clue 3: Clarify Your Cultural Lens

Make sure you believe the business case for cultural competence, and that your belief goes well beyond simple political correctness. You need to be secure enough in your belief so that you don't have to use the logic right away. If your own belief is solid, then you are willing to listen to opposing arguments because you are not threatened.

THE 7 CLUES
1. COMPANY GUIDELINES   2. LAW   3. YOUR LENS
4. CULTURAL PATTERNS   5. GROUP RADAR
6. COACH   7. ENVIRONMENT

Clue 4: Apply Cross-Cultural Patterns

Recall again the difference between Insiders and Outsiders. If you track who sees "CC" (Cultural Competence) as "PC," it is usually an Insider group in society or the organization. That is because if you are a member of the mainstream, issues related to *your* cultural group are not a problem. It's natural that you would see efforts to fix cultural problems as irrelevant—you don't have a problem! (A case before the U.S. Supreme Court to make county courthouses accessible to the disabled was brought by a man with a disability who had to crawl up the courthouse stairs, not by people who could easily climb them.)

The tendency for Insiders to be clueless about cultural issues can be predictable—or not so predictable. I have seen white people say, "There is no race problem here," at the same time people of color see it clearly. That's fairly predictable.

But members of Outsider groups on one cultural dimension can be in an Insider group on another and become surprisingly clueless. Take the case of a black controller of an organization who on the first day of a three-day session was very clear and eloquent about the barriers he had to overcome in the company because of his race. He saw the race issues (as a member of an Outsider group) clearly. "I've made it here, but it hasn't been easy. There are lots of barriers that have been put in my path. And I'm usually the only one that looks like me in the room."

The next day, when women brought up concerns related to gender, the same man (now an Insider by gender, as a man) became suddenly clueless. He hadn't seen any of these problems the women cited, and he didn't know why they were so upset. "What's the big deal? I don't think we hold women back."

So start by accepting—rather than trying to convince at the outset—that those who object to cultural competence as being PC are not seeing what you see. This may be the result of a lifetime of being in an Insider group that hasn't felt many cultural pinches. Try, then, to see what they are seeing. Get them to describe political correctness and its implications for them. Here's an example of how such a dialogue might go:

Joe: *I think this diversity stuff is a bunch of crap.*

You: *You do? Tell me about that—why so?*

Joe: *Everybody knows the company is just trying to punch a ticket and look good.*

You: *Well, it's true there have been times when it's looked like that in the past.*

Joe: *You got that right.*

THE **CLUES**   1. COMPANY GUIDELINES   2. LAW   3. YOUR LENS   4. CULTURAL PATTERNS   5. GROUP RADAR   6. COACH   7. ENVIRONMENT

You: *Sounds like this time it bothers you more, Joe. Am I right?*

Joe: *It just ticks me off—like they're saying I've got some sort of privilege compared to others.*

You: *Oh, I see. Like it diminishes what you've accomplished?*

Joe: *Yeah.*

You: *I definitely wouldn't want that. You've done a lot. I could also see if it's a company ticket punch, then that would make it a program, not something vital. Let me tell you why I think it's important to our product and our team. . . .*

▶ **Get behind people who object to diversity. See what they see.**

Behaviors, Not Beliefs

Cultural competence involves the ability to have effective dialogue—even with those who object to the emphasis on cultural competence!

You may find that people often think that the organization is trying to get them to change their *beliefs*. Make a clear distinction between behaviors and beliefs. You can reassure them that the organization is only interested in promoting *behaviors* that promote and attract all cultures.

Another aspect of effective dialogue in the workplace is the ability to disagree. Take disagreements on the topic of sexual orientation—one person believing it is an orientation that is in-born, another believing it is a choice one makes. Cultural competence doesn't insist that people change their beliefs. It *does* insist that employees work well with or provide great service to gay, lesbian, or bisexual co-workers and customers.

As a manager, you want to be able to talk with employees who believe cultural competence is PC—and to be able to disagree with that assessment. There is no need to write them off. Indeed that will get you nowhere. At the same time, you can insist on business-related behaviors—sharing information with co-workers, delighting customers—even if your employee sees a conflict in values, beliefs, or lifestyle.

▶ *Beliefs differ. Focus on behaviors.*

THE
CLUES

1. COMPANY GUIDELINES   2. LAW   3. YOUR LENS
4. CULTURAL PATTERNS   5. GROUP RADAR
6. COACH   7. ENVIRONMENT

Timing the Business Case

Once you think a person feels acknowledged and heard, you can bring out the logic for diversity:

Make the business case.   Talk about the trends toward cultural diversity among co-workers and customers, and the need for the business to respond.

Stress the need for learning.   Since exposure to, say, Africans or people with disabilities in the workplace may have been limited, all of us need to know what our assumptions are about people who are different from us. Knowing our assumptions leads to more informed, effective behavior.

Expand the definition of culture.   Particularly if you are speaking to a member of a traditionally Insider group in the United States (whites, men, Christians), think of a time when that person may have been an Outsider. Many employees have instantly become Outsider group members when their company has been bought out or merged. Employees at GTE (merged with Verizon) know clearly the experience of being one down. Others know Outsider status simply by being employees in a world where managers are the Insiders with power. In these cases, you can get people to feel more directly the need for attention to managing difference well.

Save these arguments, however, until after you have their ear.

One group of young men in a diversity training program thought that much of the company's dedication to cultural competence was PC. I didn't deny it. In some cases, they were right. Companies often do such programs just to cover a potential legal liability.

By not denying their statements, I believe I laid a foundation of trust in the beginning. They began to listen to some of the logical arguments for cultural competence later.

At the end of the day, I was surprised to hear one man say that he was going to call a co-worker right then. He had used a term for him in jest several times, and he started wondering, "Does it bother him that I use this term?" The man who had objected to political correctness was now pursuing a language issue on his own—perhaps the most politically correct aspect of cultural competence work.

▶ *If you can't beat 'em, hear 'em.*

The Wrap on Scenario 6:
The suggestions in this chapter on political correctness correspond to Clue 3: Clarify Your Cultural Lens and Clue 4: Apply Cross-Cultural Patterns.

Reluctance of "Minority" Groups to Be Open

A gay man decided he was through with hiding his sexual orientation from his work colleagues. It had become too difficult and exasperating to keep up the pretense. So he openly stated he was gay to his co-workers at a computer company.

His friend Joe watched the process. He noticed over time that his friend was not getting opportunities and assignments for which he was qualified.

Joe made his decision. He was gay, too, but he wasn't going to let his secret out.

The Business Costs of Silence

Many organizations have members of so-called minority groups who are reluctant to speak out. Joe would not reveal his sexual orientation for fear of losing opportunity. People of color fear they will be labeled as troublemakers if they talk about racial bias, so many say nothing for fear of losing opportunities. Women are often called "feminists" (read: not being objective) if they cite instances where women are treated differently from men, so they back off.

What is the cost to you and your organization of this reluctance to speak? My observation is that people still do their jobs, and still appear to be working their tails off. But what you are losing first is a sincere sense of belonging.

Reluctance to be open creates fear, uneasiness, and a feeling of resignation in a workplace. Many members of diverse cultural groups wonder, "Will my performance be undercut by my personal life?" "Am I perceived as too militant?" "Must I change who I am to the extent that it compromises my values or my essence, to the point where I want to leave, or to a degree where my work becomes drudgery?"

These are the symptoms of feeling that I don't belong. And belonging/not belonging has upside or downside consequences. Research by the Corporate Leadership Council shows the impact of employee commitment: "Highly committed employees perform up to 20 percent better than less-engaged employees and are 87 percent less likely to leave the organization than employees with low commitment."[15]

Fear, holding back, and personal compromise make for a long-term, subtle drag on performance. Employees who are anxious, fearful, or resigned lose part

THE
CLUES
7

1. COMPANY GUIDELINES   2. LAW   3. YOUR LENS
4. CULTURAL PATTERNS   5. GROUP RADAR
6. COACH   7. ENVIRONMENT

of their energy that should be devoted to work. In today's war for talent in a tight labor market, if employees leave, the cost of replacing them could run from 1.5 to 3 times their salary—between $75,000 and $150,000 for a $50,000 earner, up to $300,000 for a $100,000 earner, and so on.

People may look for a job elsewhere, or they may stay in place, but part of them doesn't want to be there. This extra energy burden is the second cost to you as a manager. You want to free that up.

The third possible cost is that you are not getting all the information you need to manage your organization. You have a skewed, unrealistic view of your workplace if you have a lot of diversity and people won't be open and honest. One African American man put it this way in a recent focus group: "You can't put issues out on the table. I don't say anything to anyone anymore."

Managers frequently tell me, in front of their people, "Oh, we don't have any problem being outspoken here." He or she looks around and everyone laughs. Don't be so sure they are laughing with you.

Cultural difference adds a new element to a scenario like this. You may not realize that people are laughing *at* you because their difference frequently holds them back. Reticence seems to be a universal pattern of cultural groups when they are not the ones in power. Not every individual in the group is reticent—indeed many are very vocal. But the reticent ones watch what happens to the vocal ones, as Joe did, and many will not speak up, thinking—"you just won't understand."

▶ *Crack the code of cultural reticence . . . and create commitment.*

Reticence Busters

If you had customers who held back suggestions that would help your business, or who didn't feel they belonged, wouldn't you hop on it? People who are reluctant to speak up are bound for greener pastures, whether customer or employee.

What can you do to ensure that cultural customers and employees feel they belong—in your business, school, or agency? Here are some practical ways to reduce the reticence to speak up:

Don't punish openness.   Learn to listen nondefensively. Sound easy? Try it when one of your employees has the courage to tell you that she thinks you have favored men, or if someone else asks you why no one but those that look like you get key assignments. Inviting openness is easy; the implementation may not be.

	1. COMPANY GUIDELINES 2. LAW 3. YOUR LENS
THE **CLUES** 7	4. CULTURAL PATTERNS 5. GROUP RADAR
	6. COACH 7. ENVIRONMENT

Use group-level radar (Clue 5). Be curious about how diverse people see the team and your behavior. Learn about their experience of the organization, which may be different as an outsider cultural group member. Doing this is a lot harder than it sounds, but it sends a strong message that honesty about perceived cultural barriers is valued because you are directly asking for feedback. Are there policies, practices, informal norms, or behaviors that have an impact on others about which you might not be aware?

Distinguish who's right from who's heard. Many times managers shut down openness because they disagree with an employee in a way that tells him "you're wrong." Try assuming cluelessness (Clue 4: Apply Cross-Cultural Patterns) regarding another person's cultural experience. You don't have to agree. You can admit that is not how you see it, but you are interested in how he does.

▶ *Cultural common sense: assume diverse people regard your organization differently.*

How Murals Demotivate

A restaurant's managers were stunned at their female employees' feedback. Women felt the expected dress, the socializing, the décor (some of which displayed nude women in Roman-type murals), and the expectations of holding back emotion all added up to a male-dominated environment that subtly demanded they be something they were not. America Online faced similar reactions in the feedback it received from women about a "boys' club" atmosphere that forced women to choose: "Will I do things I don't want to do, or potentially compromise my career?"

The cultural customers cited earlier avoided certain businesses because of the environment they perceived there. Similarly, diverse employees withhold information you need or silently look elsewhere because of work environments they experience. Here are some clues you can use in your work environment to counteract "cultural reticence":

Track. If you ask diverse employees about their experience, be alert to what they say when you check out your own organization. Who gets opportunities? Who, honestly, do you trust to carry out key projects, and are those people alike culturally: heterosexual, male or female, race, age, religion, American versus foreign born? Are there some cultural groups that are not in your organization (for example, people with disabilities)?

THE
CLUES
1. COMPANY GUIDELINES   2. LAW   3. YOUR LENS
4. CULTURAL PATTERNS   5. GROUP RADAR
6. COACH   7. ENVIRONMENT

Even if you changed nothing, *Tracking* would be useful to enable you to see what other cultural groups experience. In this way, you may be less apt to deny their claims, and thereby encourage more openness.

Catch jokes.   Jokes are one thing you can track by culture. This is covered in more detail in the next section, but jokes do have an impact on openness. So be aware if you hear jokes about particular cultural groups, and think about the potential silencing effect on members of that group.

Don't create losers.   Here is an example of facilitating when two groups see an issue very differently. Jeanne tells you that co-workers are speaking Spanish in the workplace, and they're talking about her. She wants you to tell them to stop.

You: *Well, Jeanne, I'm not going to make blanket prohibitions on speaking Spanish, but is there something that gets in the way of your work if people speak another language?*

Jeanne: *Well, no, but I do feel like they may be talking about me and I don't know.*

You: *All right, then, let's talk with [the Spanish speakers] and work that out.*

     or

> *OK, I'd like you to go speak with [the Spanish speakers] and work out something where you'll feel better about the situation. Maybe they can reassure you.*

As a manager, you are often in a position of having to make a decision. For many people, this implies coming down on one side or another. You can do this without creating losers, in many situations. In this example, you have to start by siding with the law, which doesn't allow blanket prohibitions on other languages without a business reason. You also may state that you want people to feel that they can speak their own language.

You don't, however, have to lose those who want English to be spoken.

If you have to make a decision that cuts across cultures, acknowledge both groups. In the case of Jeanne, you have not shut down the Spanish speakers, and you've begun action on Jeanne's concern.

Surprisingly, you don't always need to ignore one argument if you have decided in favor of the other. Too much energy in regard to cultural difference is spent in deciding who is right. Over time, cultural groups can feel marginalized and decide they can't

THE
CLUES
7

1. COMPANY GUIDELINES 2. LAW 3. YOUR LENS
4. CULTURAL PATTERNS 5. GROUP RADAR
6. COACH 7. ENVIRONMENT

be honest. Don't create a losing side when you don't have to.

▶ *Create wins for all groups. You'll get honesty.*

The Wrap on Scenario 7:
The suggestions in this chapter, "Reluctance of Minority Groups to Be Open," correspond to Clue 4: Apply Cross-Cultural Patterns and Clue 5: Use Group-Level Radar.

Joking

You can't joke about anything around here anymore.

Oh, so we've got to be politically correct, do we?

Managers are often in the middle when jokes are made about cultural groups. The joker says something like the statements above. Groups who are targets of the jokes voice their displeasure, or hide their resentment. You have to decide what to do.

You are also in the middle if *you* believe that there is too much political correctness about jokes. Maybe you feel you have to intervene because you are a manager, but you really think the crackdown is too much.

So let's get you out of the middle in either case. What is some of the compelling logic that will help you make your own decisions regarding jokes and their effects?

 THE CLUES

1. COMPANY GUIDELINES   2. LAW   3. YOUR LENS
4. CULTURAL PATTERNS   5. GROUP RADAR
6. COACH   7. ENVIRONMENT

Jokes and the Lost Customer

If no one could "joke about anything anymore," things would indeed be horrible. Humor is always needed in the workplace. Make this distinction, however: humor at the expense of others is one kind of humor. There is plenty of humor that doesn't denigrate someone's cultural group.

If a joke

- sends a message that a person or group is strange or incompetent

- supports stereotyping or discrimination

- puts a group "in its place"

then these statements put people down or limit them. Think about it. As a manager, you are trying to grow people, to lift them up to be their best. Jokes that put others down go precisely against one of your primary roles as a manager. They therefore can hurt the ability of your people to produce.

Jokes about cultural groups can also hurt you with customers. Of course, if you put down customers or slight their groups, you are not using the number-one customer attraction strategy. Perhaps more common, however, than directly putting down a customer is the fact that businesses lose customers because, through neglect, they appear to condone joking that includes cultural put-downs or harassment.

One of my customers had a booth at a large convention. Company representatives began joking with some of the conference attendees who visited the booth. The jokes included considerable sexual innuendo. The visitors participated in the innuendo, and the back and forth continued at length.

A representative of a large customer of this company walked by and heard this interplay. Upon returning home, the company received a letter from its customer, saying the joking was loud, unprofessional, and sexual, and it did not want to be associated with a vendor who found this behavior to be OK. The company was prepared to withdraw its considerable business, and my customer had to do considerable scrambling to keep its customer.

When you think about cultural joking, then, consider the effect of put-downs on your employees, as well as the possibility that customers could take their business elsewhere if they feel you condone put-downs of certain groups.

▶ *Get your cultural antennae up for jokes. Your employees and customers are tuned in.*

THE **CLUES**

1. COMPANY GUIDELINES   2. LAW   3. YOUR LENS
4. CULTURAL PATTERNS   5. GROUP RADAR
6. COACH   7. ENVIRONMENT

Environmental Impact Statements

The joking that was taking place in that conference booth seemed acceptable to the people participating, but the impression left on the customer was so negative that it wanted to withdraw its business. The customer was a "third party"—a very important third party—affected by joking. When you're dealing with joking issues in your workplace, you have to consider a larger field of impact. Would your customers (who are increasingly diverse) as well as your other employees appreciate the joke you just heard?

With the third party impact in mind, here is your backup when you have to intervene with jokes.

Clue 7: Build a Cross-Cultural Environment

This is one of the primary Clues you are using to prevent problems and encourage a great workplace. Decide the kind of environment you want. If you want to lift up people, then you don't want jokes about people's cultural groups.

Remember that many Outsiders will not speak up. That means you have to account for impact that may be occurring without your knowing it. Consider the following scenario:

In a group exercise I led with defense industry employees, one man said, "I've looked into the research on sexual orientation. Are you all aware of what the research says?"

At that moment, the other four men in the group simultaneously slid their chairs away from their colleague, laughing. Their nonverbal message: "Ooh, could he be gay? Let's back away from this guy."

But what is the greater concern here? It's the potential impact on your workplace. Any gay or lesbian person watching this action by the four men is likely to conclude, "OK, I've got to make sure no one knows I'm gay."

The complaint about sexual orientation is often, "Why does anyone need to advertise their sexual orientation anyway?" They don't. But even without advertising, the gay or lesbian person in this organization is given a clear message: You must make extra effort to keep your sexual orientation hidden. Think of all the extra energy that must therefore be spent at work on hiding something: no pictures of your partner, no partner at a work social function, being careful around all conversations involving weekends and social activities—the list is long.

Perhaps the "don't ask, don't tell" policy forces this on some military organizations. If you're not subject to that policy, however, you don't want someone having to be so careful at the workplace.

THE
CLUES
7

1. COMPANY GUIDELINES   2. LAW   3. YOUR LENS
4. CULTURAL PATTERNS   5. GROUP RADAR
6. COACH   7. ENVIRONMENT

In the case of the defense industry guys, you can stop the action and ask the four:

Why the movement backing away?

Stay with the question if they stall. Once you get some answers close to the truth, explain:

You know, I want to make sure that everyone feels welcome here, and that people don't have to spend mental energy covering up their lives.

You could suggest to the four:

Let's talk about what we think the impact on those who are gay could be.

Have a discussion.

The negative impact of joking on your work environment is certainly not limited to sexual orientation. Jokes and put-downs are made about the foods people heat up in microwaves, reflecting their national culture. Do you want people fearing ridicule because of that? There are jokes about age groups, women, races, and regions of the country people represent. Go beyond political correctness debates. You have bigger responsibilities.

▶ ***Plan for cultural jokes. Think about the kind of workplace you want.***

Joke Backup

Let's say you're clear about where cultural jokes fit in the kind of environment for diversity you are trying to build. You should also know the law (Clue 2). Joking can be harassment if it is unwelcome and repeated, coming under the hostile work environment definition put forward by the EEOC.

Recall the protected classes that come under the purview of civil rights legislation and antidiscrimination law. You can't discriminate against religious and national origin groups, so making jokes about these groups or their language, foods, or customs can be seen as harassment of a person based on their group. Of course, the same applies for other protected classes, such as racial groups, women, people with disabilities, and people over 40.

It is likely that your company backs this up with language in its policies that prohibits this kind of harassment. You might check out that language. Many of my customers have stronger protections than federal or state law; for example, prohibiting discrimination or harassment based on sexual orientation. Some states include this stipulation, but not all.

All companies, of course, want to avoid damaging lawsuits. Most, however, have another motivation that relates to the purpose of the laws. They want their employees to be as productive as possible, so they don't want anyone concerned about whether they will be harassed. They also don't want their customers thinking they condone put-downs of cultural groups.

Sometimes, however, employers don't know what their diverse employees feel or fear regarding expressions of their culture that might draw derision. Be aware. As a manager of a diverse workforce, it's up to you to be the company representative that is clear about the effect of cultural jokes.

▶ *Know the spirit of the law. Get out of the middle on jokes.*

The Wrap on Scenario 8:
The suggestions in this chapter on joking correspond to Clue 7: Build a Cross-Cultural Environment and Clue 2: Turn to the Law.

"I'm Not Prejudiced. My Parents Raised Me to Be Colorblind"

This may be the most common statement I hear in cultural diversity training sessions or in social settings when the topic of cultural difference comes up. Why are statements like these an issue for you as a manager?

Because you need openness to build a culturally competent business or organization. Openness to diversity attracts diverse customers and the best employees.

The Best Diversity Measure

Many times, those who are the most open to diversity are those who are also open to introspection. They consider what past and present actions may tell them about their cultural competence.

On the other hand, don't your suspicions get raised when you hear statements like these?

| THE 7 CLUES | 1. COMPANY GUIDELINES 2. LAW 3. YOUR LENS
4. CULTURAL PATTERNS 5. GROUP RADAR
6. COACH 7. ENVIRONMENT |

"Your President is not a crook."
— President Richard Nixon

"I did not have sex with that woman."
— President Bill Clinton

"I didn't do it, Mommy."
— Four-year-old child

In the same way, it is most often the people who say "I'm not prejudiced" who give me pause, because they often turn out to be the least open.

Your problem as a manager in a diverse world is not bias. Everyone has bias. Your problem is employees who are not skilled across cultures, and cultural skill is based on openness.

Here are some of the obstacles that accrue from close-mindedness about one's own behavior regarding culture:

Devaluing diversity. Time and again, managers of diversity efforts in organizations tell me that the biggest block to having the organization value the diversity of employees and customers is the people who see no need for attention to diversity.

Devaluing customers. Customers who feel their cultural affiliation is affecting their treatment can hit a brick wall with arguments from your employees who deny any possibility of the influence of cultural factors.

Devaluing co-workers. Those who think they have no bias discount employees who experience the influence of cultural factors on interactions, recruitment, promotion, or customers. In fact, many employees who cite the influence of culture say they are made out to be crazy by managers or fellow employees who summarily dismiss culture. They are often seen as making excuses or being "too sensitive."

The commonality in these cases is this: close-mindedness blocks your efforts to attract more customers in a diverse world, or develop a workplace where all of today's varied workforce thrives.

▶ *Measure cultural openness. It's having impact.*

Beyond Parents

So what do you do to encourage openness, particularly when someone insists, "I'm not prejudiced!"

There are some logical responses that can work with some people, but remember that likely there is emotion below this denial of bias. Logic usually doesn't

THE
CLUES
7
1. COMPANY GUIDELINES   2. LAW   3. YOUR LENS
4. CULTURAL PATTERNS   5. GROUP RADAR
6. COACH   7. ENVIRONMENT

"*I had good parents, too. . . . And a TV. And a neighborhood . . .*"

work if the problem is emotion (thank you, Peter Block, for that reminder).[16] So try the logic, and if that doesn't work, address the emotional side, too. Here are some of the Clues to use.

Clue 6: Coach Performance Cross-Culturally

On the logical side, you can tell your employee that you are glad that his or her parents gave him that message. Now go for the expansion of mindset that coaching promotes.

Add that parents are not the only source of cultural messages. You can acknowledge the person's upbringing and simply differ by explaining your experience:

You know, you're right. I don't recall my parents ever saying anything against cultural groups. I'm trying to think of how they went about their daily lives. For example, I know they never hung out with people of other races, so I didn't have an actual model of relating to other races as everyday friends and colleagues.

I also consider other cultural influences besides my parents. A lot of my early thinking was influenced by TV. I don't recall ever seeing people with disabilities in leading roles, and most of the Latino roles were pretty ridiculous characters, like Jose Jimenez.

We learn which cultures have power positions or good jobs through role models. What race and gender were the professional people in your neighborhood, or who were the financially successful ones? In mine, they were virtually all white men.

My parents never said anything against other groups, but the absence or portrayal of those cultural groups spoke louder. What was your experience?

▶ **Teach culture beyond parents. Be your own example.**

THE **CLUES**

1. COMPANY GUIDELINES   2. LAW   3. YOUR LENS
4. CULTURAL PATTERNS   5. GROUP RADAR
6. COACH   7. ENVIRONMENT

The Backfire of Zero Tolerance

A middle school is in the news because some of the children report being the target of racial slurs. The principal declares there will be "zero tolerance" for these statements.[17]

No doubt the principal must intervene, just as any manager must if culturally-related slurs are used. But if you have employees declaring, "I'm not prejudiced," and you feel they are just a bit too strident, you may be hearing fears, defensiveness, or anxiety about zero tolerance. Most organizations tend to imply "zero" even if they don't state it. So how do you get to the emotions behind "I'm not prejudiced," when an organization's messages about diversity may put some people on eggshells?

Start by adjusting your expectations. As a manager, you are *not* expecting that people have no bias. It constantly amazes me that participants enter diversity training sessions thinking I expect cultural purity. I believe they think this because their organizations and managers have drilled into them a legalistic zero tolerance for discrimination.

Avoiding discriminatory *actions* is possible. Avoiding biased *reactions* or *feelings* is virtually impossible. I grew up in an all-white town. I notice that I feel uncomfortable or more alert when I am in a predominantly black neighborhood. That's a biased reaction, influenced by my background.

I assume that my early experience is not going away. It happened. I can't say "I'm not prejudiced." I soaked in my surroundings, just like everyone else. But I can influence my actions.

The odd, paradoxical truth is that the best way to keep my actions from being biased is to accept my biased reactions. If I am conscious that I can be prejudiced and acknowledge it, I am less likely to act jumpy or fearful around blacks. I'm not hiding anything.

Now, if I insist that I have no bias, I am not allowing my discomfort to be conscious. I'm not aware that I am making myself anxious. In a work situation, I'm more likely to think that a black person glared at me, or didn't smile enough, or wasn't friendly, if I am not conscious of the part my own anxiety plays in the interaction.

You want your employees to be "emotionally intelligent" about culture. To the person who insists they are not biased, you can help him clarify his cultural attitudes by the set of more expansive questions about background that were just discussed. And you can clarify that bias is natural. Zero tolerance of discriminatory actions shouldn't be allowed to interfere with

THE
CLUES

1. COMPANY GUIDELINES   2. LAW   3. YOUR LENS
4. CULTURAL PATTERNS   5. GROUP RADAR
6. COACH   7. ENVIRONMENT

learning that will help your employees treat diverse customers and employees with greater skill.

▶ *Don't let zero tolerance encourage denial.*

"I'm Not Prejudiced"
Meets the Customer

A Georgia state representative explains matter-of-factly, "Believe me, . . . in my travels through the government buildings, I know my white colleagues are treated differently than me."[18]

If a state representative complained to one of your employees that he had been treated differently because of his race, would you want your employee to respond, "I'm not prejudiced. My parents raised me to be color-blind!"?

The point of learning about cultural diversity is to open up the natural lack of awareness one experiences by not being a member of a particular cultural group. Speak about *Clueless Majorities* and *Denial* to your employees (see Clue 4). You want people to be receptive if a customer complains, rather than responding with knee-jerk denial. You can make openness about bias OK by reassuring them that you don't expect them to be bias-free—no one is.

Tell your employees that it is natural to deny that culture could be involved in one's interactions. In our society, it has become a major taboo to be seen as having bias toward anyone regarding race, gender, disability, religion—you name it. But you can't let that taboo censor people's honesty with themselves. They don't necessarily have to make an outward confession; they do need to skillfully react to customer or fellow employee perceptions in this global world.

▶ *Teach cultural customer service. Don't deny customer cultural perceptions.*

The Wrap on Scenario 9:
The suggestions in this chapter on prejudice correspond to Clue 6: Coach Performance Cross-Culturally, Clue 4: Apply Cross-Cultural Patterns, and Clue 3: Clarify Your Cultural Lens.

THE
CLUES

1. COMPANY GUIDELINES   2. LAW   3. YOUR LENS
4. CULTURAL PATTERNS   5. GROUP RADAR
6. COACH   7. ENVIRONMENT

SCENARIO | 1 0

Cultural Conflicts about Conflict

A friend who, several times, had to conduct trips with Asian businessmen, felt that men from India were abrupt and rude when conflicts arose involving her and others. I am certain there are individual Indian men who are not that way (we only need to think of Gandhi), but to an outsider to the culture, this is how she saw that group's approach to conflict.

Conflict in a multicultural world is often about *how* we actually handle conflict rather than the conflict itself. "He gets in my face! I hate that!" "She goes behind my back—doesn't come to me directly." Here are some suggestions when you manage diverse people who differ in how they resolve conflict.

Not My Style

A colleague who has worked overseas speaks of the ineffectiveness of the American style of giving direct feedback in Asia. She found much more success receiving and giving feedback when it was done through a trusted third party. Whether you or your employees are in the conflict, identify how everyone involved prefers to deal with it.

Most people don't think about this. Some may say simply, "I don't like conflict—I avoid it." That's better awareness than nothing. It's a preference, and it influences how that person judges someone else who deals with conflict differently. If you don't enjoy conflict—and you have a partner who confronts differences more easily—you might think the person was regularly jumping on you. Since you enjoy it so little, it might seem like it's happening a lot.

Without knowing your own conflict style, anyone who uses a style you don't like is likely to get blamed for being wrong, or "abrupt and rude," or "too emotional." This furthers the conflict because now we are not only talking about the issue in dispute, we're talking about the way someone goes about talking about the issue.

If you know your preferred style of dealing with conflict, you are much more likely to accept your style as a preference, not the universally right way to do things. Let's take a classic male-female example. Some women say they cry when they are upset or in an argument. Men who haven't thought about this might reflect for a moment. When a woman cries, or if you are

THE **7 CLUES**   1. COMPANY GUIDELINES   2. LAW   3. YOUR LENS   4. CULTURAL PATTERNS   5. GROUP RADAR   6. COACH   7. ENVIRONMENT

in a conflict with a woman and she uses much more feeling than you, how do you feel, honestly?

Are you comfortable with it—that is, able to respond to the situation with calmness and appropriate emotion? Or are you frozen, not knowing what to do or wishing this would get over as fast as possible? Do you respond awkwardly or say, "Let's talk about this later," and skip out of there? Or do you simply conclude, "This woman's being too emotional"? In the case of "A Restaurant for Men?" (Clue 6), that conclusion was the data point cited for keeping a female waiter from being promoted.

Here's another way to go. Think first about how *you* prefer to handle conflict. Maybe you

- prefer laying out the facts first

- like competing to win

- have trouble identifying a feeling (other than anger)

With any of those preferences, dealing with emotion first is not your strong suit. It's possible that you see a woman's emotions magnified beyond where they really are because using emotion is not your particular comfort zone.

So "clarify your cultural lens"—examining the method of resolving conflict that got passed down to you—is a must in working out differences across culture. As a man, I believe I did get a message passed down about emotion. It was, and still is, when I am with men: Don't be too emotional. Gender, of course, is not the only "culture forming" part of us, so consider, for example, how conflict was handled in your family, or in the region or country you come from, or in the military, if you are a military person.

▶ *Clarify your conflict style—and get your employees to do the same.*

Digging In

In attempting to resolve cultural conflicts, acknowledge the fact that conflict styles may influence the situation. Here are two ways to do that:

Talk directly about the styles. If you have clarified your own preferred way of handling conflict, you are prepared to talk about it. Tell your counterpart how you tend to go about solving conflicts. If you are the manager facilitating a conflict, ask the two people to identify their styles. You might go so far as to ask if there is a cultural difference in the preferred styles. This

THE	1. COMPANY GUIDELINES 2. LAW 3. YOUR LENS
CLUES	4. CULTURAL PATTERNS 5. GROUP RADAR
	6. COACH 7. ENVIRONMENT

puts one of the unspoken influences on the conflict on the table.

Match the other's style.   Effectiveness with other cultures involves growth—increasing your range of skills. Now that you know your preference, and the style of the other, try matching her style. If feelings are not your bag, but your counterpart uses emotion openly, try going with her strength for a while.

You might ask the other person to tell you the impact of the conflict on her emotions; for example, "So, when I said what I said, what was the impact on you emotionally?"

Then try her style out for yourself. Try identifying your emotion. Find it and name it. Use nuance. Instead of saying, "I'm angry," use the range of "mad" emotions. Maybe you're frustrated rather than angry, or disappointed, or upset, shocked, or envious.

Matching on style may help you resolve the actual dispute. Many times people are more upset about the *way* someone conducted himself or herself than they are about the actual issue. When the style issue is resolved, it is amazing how many times the actual dispute seems small or petty.

You may have had the same experience. When the conflict is resolved, the actual resolution seems so simple that the "big" conflict can seem almost trifling. Warring departments finally work out their differences by deciding to meet once a month to keep each other updated. A savvy support person has been regularly resisted by a manager she serves, so she invites him to lunch, they establish a better relationship, and the resistance goes away.

To be sure, it's not always that easy; but one of the reasons it's not is the frequent drama and resentment that builds up. Prevent the drama by

- knowing your own style

- realizing that another culture may have a different style

- making those styles conscious

- maybe even trying to improve yourself

▶ *In conflicts about conflict approaches, talk about the approaches . . . and try expanding yours.*

Your Nobel Peace Prize

One customer reported that among her international workforce, she dealt with physical fights and refusals

	THE	1. COMPANY GUIDELINES 2. LAW 3. YOUR LENS
CLUES		4. CULTURAL PATTERNS 5. GROUP RADAR
		6. COACH 7. ENVIRONMENT

to work together among Africans who lived in the United States but brought their national or ethnic conflicts with them.

In part one, I mentioned that this was a brave new world for managers. But no one told you that you needed to be the Secretary General of the United Nations. Even the Secretary and his U.N. colleagues aren't doing so well on historical conflicts that have been brought into the everyday workplace.

So how are you as a manager supposed to handle age-old cultural conflicts?

Begin by refusing to accept the Nobel Peace Prize. Lower any expectation that you will clear up problems between the Hutus and the Tutsis of Rwanda, the Indians and Pakistanis, or Republicans and Democrats, for that matter.

Then use your power in the workplace. Start by going back to Clue 1: Look to Your Organization's Cultural Guidelines. Your team and your organization have certain expectations for task performance and for cooperation across many lines, cultural among them. So you can use those guidelines to insist that delighting the customer and employee teamwork are job requirements. Link cross-cultural cooperation to these goals.

Your organization's guidelines provide a foundation for managing these kind of historical conflicts. So, too, does the work you have done on Clue 7. You build a cross-cultural environment where inclusion is "in" and exclusion is "out."

These backdrops give you leverage when you have to dig in to the details of a historical cultural conflict. When you have waded through the particulars, as a bottom line use the distinction mentioned earlier between beliefs and behaviors. You can tell the warring factions that the company does not expect them to change their *beliefs* about someone else; however, the organization can expect them to *behave* in a way that supports its primary goals.

A customer of mine had a conflict with a Muslim doctor who was less than respectful of women staff. She has focused more on establishing, with the team, core team principles of cooperation, and a bit less on hammering at the interpersonal dynamic.

There is a good deal of research that shows that large organizations or communities can promote success by acknowledging past conflicts sincerely, but not dwelling on them. The way out is by focusing on a common, compelling future.[19]

When the time is right, consider this kind of future focus for your cultural conflicts. Outright battles and refusals to cooperate are simply intolerable in the workplace. They certainly require your facilitation skill to calm down the situation. But your ultimate solution

THE
CLUES
1. COMPANY GUIDELINES   2. LAW   3. YOUR LENS
4. CULTURAL PATTERNS   5. GROUP RADAR
6. COACH   7. ENVIRONMENT

may not be to solve the conflict, but to refocus it with the leverage provided by organizational goals and guidelines.

▶ *Preach peace, but focus on goals.*

The Wrap on Scenario 10:
The suggestions in this chapter on cultural conflicts correspond to Clue 3: Clarify Your Cultural Lens, Clue 5: Use Group-Level Radar, and Clue 1: Look to Your Organization's Cultural Guidelines.

PART FOUR

Summing
It All Up

The Outsider Gap

You join a discussion regarding a racial incident, and you are the only one of your race among 20 people. You live for a year in a country where you don't speak the language. You are sent to interview a man who is deaf. You are the only woman—again—in a meeting with 10 men, establishing strategy and budget for the year. You enter a club and find you are the only heterosexual in the place, and people are looking at you.

Maybe in the din and frenzy of modern life, situations like this pop up for you only as occasional episodes, leaving a feeling of fear, discomfort, embarrassment, or even challenge, but remaining a blip. For other readers of this book, being aware of your difference from the crowd is very frequent and palpable.

There have always been gaps like these, where one's experience of the world differs dramatically from others. But in the workplace today, not acknowledging that gap—or outright contempt for those who do experience being different culturally—can have consequences. Poor cross-cultural skills or policies can mean everything from large lawsuits, to customers choosing someone else's business, to your employee deciding to plow ahead, performing adequately, but with little commitment to your organization.

Cluelessness—not knowing what you don't know about how your customers and employees see you and your organization—looks more like a threat to survival every day, as customers and decision makers become more diverse racially, by gender, by age group, by physical ability, by religion, and so on.

This cultural gap—some feeling clearly like an Outsider, others not seeing that experience at all—influences business success. A potential customer of mine feels like the lone wolf crying out to his large company to recognize the demographic change that is there. Sixty percent of the company's employees in one state don't speak English; less than 2 percent of the managers speak their language. That's one indicator of the arrival of the brave new world of part one. How would you like to be one of the brave new managers?

Tuning in the World . . . and You

It is an odd thing to speak around the country to many people who are not as convinced as I am that difference makes a difference. Regularly, I'm told, "We all get along. Nobody has any problems."

Then I recall that Cambodians are driving around our hospital parking lots refusing to ask security guards for directions; young defense company engineers aren't telling their headquarters' counterparts that they are looking elsewhere because they are consistently told to just go along; black men are choosing to remain silent so as not to be seen as "rattling cages."

Cluelessness lives. There is a great deal we don't know that we don't know about the diverse people we manage, the customers we serve, and the children we teach. That's why so much of this book is about activating your own cultural radar. Know yourself—culturally. Look for the patterns that repeat. Add the group level of awareness to your repertoire as a leader.

All of these suggestions are things that can be done every day, without expenditure or a training program. In fact, now that you have your cultural lens on, use the best training program we've got: the news, the newspaper, and your community (workplace or home). Tune in the world.

When you spend time *Tracking* everyday events, you see cultural patterns more clearly. As I was writing this book, examples just popped off the pages of newspapers and out of people's mouths. Your commitment to leading diverse people and understanding cultural difference sharpens if the radar is turned on.

Somewhere in the seriousness, you also find fun. You discover much more about your colleagues and friends. You gain a greater diversity of friends, who challenge your way of being. You grow.

Learning about cultural difference also inevitably, and in one way surprisingly, brings you back to yourself. You discover preferences, and deepen your effectiveness as you gain comfort with your background and your foibles. You tune in to you.

Would that our leaders and our organizations discover the same, for the sake of our employees, customers, and fellow human beings. Counter cultural cluelessness—crack the cultural code.

NOTES

1. Dernovsek, Darla. "Serving Hispanic Members." *Credit Union Magazine* 67 (2001): 62–67.

2. Kahn, Ric. "Ethiopian Immigrants Use Boston Garages As Their Path to Good Life." *Boston Globe*, Apr. 14, 2002.

3. www.merck.com/about/diversity/employee_diversity/div_competitive_more.html

4. Pierce, Chester. "Irascible Behaviors in Black Managers." *American Journal of Orthopsychiatry* (1971). *Quoted in* Ray, LeRoi R., Jr. "Black Studies: A Discussion of Evaluation." *Journal of Negro Education* 45 (1976): 391. *See also* Delgado, Richard and Stefancic, Jean. *Critical Race Theory: An Introduction.* New York: New York University Press, 2001.

5. Frost, Delyte D. "Dialogue with Difference.™" 1984, 1996.

6. "Women, Minorities Feel Left Out at AOL." *Washington Post,* Sept. 27, 2003.

7. Credit and Trademark goes to the consulting organization, Elsie Y. Cross Associates, Philadelphia, PA for this term.

8. "They Open More Doors for Women." *Washington Post,* Feb. 4, 2007.

9. Daniels, Aubrey C. *Bringing Out the Best in People.* New York: McGraw Hill, 2000.

10. Thanks to my colleague, Xavier Espinosa (Cultural Resources Coordinator, St. Joseph's Hospital, Orange County, CA), for this concept.

11. "Women, Minorities Feel Left Out at AOL." *Washington Post,* Sept. 27, 2003.

12. Beckwith, Harry. *Selling the Invisible.* (1997); *The Invisible Touch.* (2000). New York: Warner Books.

13. "They Open More Doors for Women," *Washington Post,* Feb. 4, 2007.

14. "Women, Minorities Feel Left Out at AOL," *Washington Post,* Sept. 27, 2003.

15. www.careerjournal.com/myc/diversity/20021028-bennett. html

16. Block, Peter. *Flawless Consulting.* Austin, Tex.: Jossey-Bass/ Pfeiffer, 2000.

17. "School's parents concerned about racial slurs," nbc4.com, Apr. 7, 2006.

18. "McKinney Apologizes over Scuffle with Officers." *Washington Post,* Apr. 7, 2006.

19. Marvin Weisbord popularized this research in his book, *Discovering Common Ground,* San Francisco: Berrett-Koehler Publishers, 1992.

ACKNOWLEDGMENTS

Having read this book, I hope you would agree on how vital the person is who

▶ said, "You could make that a book." Judith Leibowitz

▶ recommended, "I'll read an installment at the end of each week," and thereby birthed the book. My dear Kathleen

▶ edited, and tolerated, her son-in-law. Ann Bruen, uncommon mother-in-law

▶ labored over reading early manuscripts. Senator Janet Howell, Elita Christiansen, Tiane Mitchell Gordon, Carolyn Jones, Alexandra Merrill, Marvin Weisbord, Sandra Evers-Manly, Sid Fuchs, Peter Norlin, Kristen Taylor, Dr. Edith Jones, Teressa Griffin, Jeff Robbins, Janice Bozzi, Robin Fenner, Judith Leibowitz, Supervisor Catherine Hudgins, Dr. James Garvin

▶ shows up so often here. Peter Norlin, you always show up for me and the world. Thank you.

▶ showed me the way with her book, *Seal the Deal,* a book for growing your professional service, and gave constant help. Suzi Pomerantz

▶ put my own cultural story in the logo. Michele Keen

▶ edited content with grace and showed us "real" food in Austin. Leslie Stephen

▶ edited detail with grace. Deborah Costenbader

▶ reminded me this was good. Peter Norlin, Alexandra Merrill, Michele Keen, Jeff Robbins

▶ designed in style. Suzanne Pustejovsky-Perry

▶ answered my "please help—fast!" questions, regularly and without complaint. Sheila Haji, Wendy Conklin, Peter Norlin, Kathleen Finn, Carolyn Jones, Peter Bopp, Maxine Fuller, John and Kathy Baker, Kent and Jeanne Harvey

▶ wrote the great books whose format I followed, and generously offered feedback on the title. Harry Beckwith

▶ played the "clued-in" customer. Thank you, Carolyn Jones, Elita Christiansen, Martine Charles, Tony Patterson, Judy McFarland

▶ in developing my thinking and feeling, played the role of colleague like Oscar nominees. Winners for skill, comedy, love, and friendship: Teressa Griffin, Sheila Haji, Maxine Fuller, Judith Leibowitz, Peter Norlin, Bill Woodson, Anne Litwin, Duane Wade, Julie Pierce-Williams, Dorinda Capole, Toni Dunton-Butler, Lee Butler, Jennifer Powell, Angela Watts, Sara Keenan-Rohling, Carolyn Jones, Lauren Nile. Thanks also to the Elsie Y. Cross network.

▶ kept asking, with unfailing excitement, "How's the book?" Lee Thompson, Jeff Robbins, Sara Keenan-Rohling, Rob and Paula Angell, Terry Redican, Ron Castaldi

▶ lent her producer mind and many hours to cover copy for her brother, and perhaps failed with her maxim, "Cut, cut, cut!" Joan Finn Adkison

▶ became a book title consultant. Everyone, including the Finns, Wexlers, Bakers, Corkeys, Mark and Nancy Velez (Many of these also ultimately failed . . . but valiantly!)

▶ drew. Revised. Drew. Revised . . . and without complaining. Chris Velez

▶ invited me to add another family to the one I love. Jeff Robbins, the Angells, all the Bruens, and Sunny Sharma and all the Sharmas

▶ lives the course on positive living (lucky me). Kathleen Finn, my love

▶ gave the course on passion. My father, Bill Finn

THE AUTHOR

Tom Finn consults to leaders and organizations that face global pressure. The ideas in this book focus on the "global" aspect of his work, whether one's business is multinational or local, facing challenges that arise from multicultural workforces and constituents in communities, schools, agencies, or firms.

With his colleague, Peter Norlin, Tom also addresses the "pressure" side of business today. His LifeLine Consulting Services increase leaders' capacity for situations where heavy responsibility and overload threaten an organization's sales and profits, new product generation, customer service, and employee health.

Tom's corporate career began at St. Luke's Episcopal/Texas Children's Hospitals in Houston, and continued for eight years at Westinghouse. There he consulted to internal and external customers on all aspects of organizational effectiveness before starting his consulting firm in 1991.

Tom has consulted to leaders and teams of all levels in the United States, South America, Central America, and Asia for over twenty years. He has helped organizations plan their futures, align employees in common commitments, and overcome conflicts that hurt the business. Some of Tom's customers have included Booz | Allen | Hamilton, ETrade Financial, General Dynamics Land Systems, Inova Health Systems, Texaco, Verizon, The World Bank, and the Argentine Education Ministry.

Tom is a graduate of Brown University in Providence, Rhode Island, and received his MS in International Business from Georgetown University. He is fluent in Spanish and conducts consulting and training in that language when needed. He has also studied Russian.

Tom lives in Reston, Virginia with his wife Kathleen. He can be contacted directly at info@lifelineconsulting.com.

ABOUT TFA, INC.

Tom Finn Associates, Inc. (TFA) provides leadership, team, and organization development consulting services. TFA specializes in assisting leaders in high-pressure roles and multicultural settings.

In the area of diversity management, TFA helps organizations and leaders

✓ discover diverse customers

✓ improve their service to current multicultural customers

✓ retain diverse talent

✓ attract multicultural talent by creating an environment that champions diversity.

For information about consulting or presentations related to managing diversity, contact TFA at info@areyouclueless.com.

TFA offers specialized leadership development for leaders with heavy responsibility and high-pressure jobs through its LifeLine Consulting Services. LifeLine's research shows business is losing sales, product ideas, employee talent, and effective customer service due to unaddressed overload in the workplace.

LifeLine uses personal biography as a tool to build influence over business challenges that are baffling, chronic, or stuck. Information on LifeLine can be found at www.lifelineconsulting.com. Contact Tom at info@lifelineconsulting.com.

YOUR CLUELESS STORIES

Do you have a clueless story? A scenario where an organization is "not getting" how attention to cultural difference can grow the business, attract or keep talent, or solve a problem?

Or can you relate a story when you were clueless about race, gender, sexual orientation, disability, language, nationality, or some other aspect of cultural diversity?

All of us can be clueless about culture. If we get the stories out there, more leaders and communities can see the impact of our multicultural world and use that awareness for optimism, new business, and problem solving. Tell us your clueless stories. If there's a success story in there, let us know. We will post scenarios on our website. Go to www.areyouclueless.com to submit your story.

FSC
Mixed Sources
Product group from well-managed
forests and other controlled sources

Cert no. SW-COC-002283
www.fsc.org
© 1996 Forest Stewardship Council